1989

Breaking Silence

Breaking Silence

A Family Grows with Deafness

Ferne Pellman Glick
and
Donald R. Pellman

Foreword by McCay Vernon

HERALD PRESS
Scottdale, Pennsylvania
Kitchener, Ontario
1982

Library of Congress Cataloging in Publication Data

Glick, Ferne Pellman, 1933-
  Breaking silence.

  1. Children, Deaf—Family relationships. I. Pellman,
Donald R., 1942-   II. Title.
HV2392.2.G55   362.8'2   82-6067
ISBN 0-8361-1999-1   AACR2
ISBN 0-8361-3300-5 (pbk.)

BREAKING SILENCE
Copyright © 1982 by Herald Press, Scottdale, Pa. 15683
  Published simultaneously in Canada by Herald Press
  Kitchener, Ont. N2G 4M5
Library of Congress Catalog Card Number: 82-6067
International Standard Book Numbers:
  0-8361-1999-1 (hardcover)
  0-8361-3300-5 (paperback)
Design by Alice B. Shetler

82 83 84 85 86 87 88 12 11 10 9 8 7 6 5 4 3 2 1

To the Glick and Pellman families,
with all their extensions,
the people who always heard us
even when we didn't know what to say.

Foreword

There is a credibility when parents who have successfully raised deaf children write about their experiences which exists with no other authors. The Glicks faced the unusual challenge of twins, both of whom were born deaf.

The obstacles of inadequate services, bureaucratic indifference, conflicting professional views, and the multitude of other issues involved in raising deaf children all confronted the Glicks. These experiences are related in fascinating, frank, often heartrending fashion. Parents and professionals in deafness will find a gold mine of insights in this book, but even more important these pages reflect a rather basic statement of the human condition. *Breaking Silence* has a generality far beyond deafness per se. *Breaking Silence* is unique among books about deaf children in that it presents the issues but leaves the readers to make their own decisions.

Few who start this book will put it down without having grown in their understanding of deafness and family life.

McCay Vernon, PhD
Editor, *American Annals of the Deaf*

Breaking Silence

Chapter 1

Everything was all right. The twins, Craig and Carson, were sitting on opposite sides of the fence, their hands over their ears, howling "oo . . . oo . . . oo" and rocking back and forth in the peculiar way they had developed early in life. Everything was all right. But twins certainly had strange habits, I thought, and turned from the kitchen window back to my pie with a smile and a sense of pleasure in those two solid eighteen-month-old bodies, the straight, blue eyes, and the two heads that had made two almost identical impressions on our world.

The fence was a great relief to me. It divided the backyard into equal parts, giving each boy his own place to run so that I didn't have to worry about their biting each other for a while. Biting was one of the less attractive features they had developed—at ten weeks—along with strong sets of teeth. But you learned to cope with twins, I thought. You learned to prop bottles and rock two armfuls at once and put up fences if it came to that.

Vernon was a practical man, good at inventing things like

the fence. When he put up a fence, it was straight. I hoped he wouldn't come home too late, although I knew he wouldn't leave the work on his father's farm next door until everyone else had quit. I hoped, too, he wouldn't be glum tonight, radiating a silence that asked why the boys were so wild, why another lamp had been broken, why I was too exhausted to set the twins straight. Vernon had moods. But he also had a sense of humor and had come up with most of the phrases with which we laughed off our troubles. "Their guardian angels must have ulcers!" he'd say when the boys had had some narrow escape. Vernon wasn't afraid to change diapers either, and he rocked the boys to sleep at night. I looked above the sink to a varnished slice of pine that said in a heavy script: "Kwitcherbellyakin." We would cope.

The telephone rang. The voice on the other end had the broad, warm Pennsylvania Dutch accent of the Mennonite community where we lived. It was the woman next door, a good neighbor and mother of eight well-behaved children. "Just thought you might like to know—the boys have taken all their clothes off again!" The voice was full of good humor that covered, almost, a faint touch of alarm.

Out in the muggy afternoon the naked boys were racing along the fence, grabbing at each other through the wire mesh and jabbering in the private language they seemed to understand between themselves. I called to them but got no response. They ran to the other end of the yard, where I cornered them, one at a time, and pulled on their suits again. They screamed and fought, but I got the straps on and pinned them as best I could, knowing full well there was no combination the boys couldn't undo in a minute. I went back inside and through the window could see them sitting on the ground, taking everything apart in stubborn concentration. "Like little animals" was the thought that

12

Chapter 2

The lights stayed lit all night on September 2, 1956, in the isolated fishing village of Baie Verte, Newfoundland, when Craig and Carson were born. Everyone knew I was in labor because the electric generator did not shut off at the accustomed hour of midnight. This time it went on and on, humming its accompaniment to my pain as I lay in a stark room of the local clinic, wondering if there would be triplets or just twins.

"Must be the new teacher's wife," the villagers mumbled to each other in their beds, and laughed. My improbable shape had been a growing cause for local amusement.

Craig was born at one in the morning. They put him in the pink incubator, powered with a light bulb, that Vernon had carefully constructed in case any of our unpredictable number of infants would be born prematurely. But Craig promptly kicked off the glass top of the box and bellowed that he was ready for the real world outside.

For the next five hours I lay waiting on the delivery table while the doctor and Vernon nervously drank coffee and told hunting stories, until finally at six o'clock Carson was born.

"Are there any more?" I asked wearily. Both boys weighed exactly six pounds, ten ounces, and were perfectly healthy. Reassured that my waiting was over, I managed to smile at the coincidence: my babies were born on Labor Day.

"I really felt sorry for you last night," Vernon said in the gray morning light. "I wish I could have helped more." We felt very close. Married at 19 and 21, we had been childless for five years and were now eager for a family. Adding to the general air of celebration surrounding our double birth on that day was the village's annual custom of going out to pick blueberries on the "burnovers."

We did have some quick lessons in our new responsibilities. The next day, because the clinic had become crowded with two more women and their babies, I needed to take charge of the twins. The nurse would check in as she could to see how we were faring.

That same day also marked Vernon's first experience as a teacher. A conscientious objector, he had been sent to Newfoundland to teach school under the Voluntary Service Program of the Mennonite Church and the United Church of Canada. He had never taught before and had received no teacher training. Now he was caught between his first set of papers and his first batch of dirty diapers.

Neither of us can remember ever being rested in those early days of parenthood. When the twins were six months old, we moved into the teacherage with another young couple—where our quarters were still cramped, Vernon was overworked, and I had to do a lot of cooking and cleaning. Fortunately, we were young and took it all as an adventure.

"Wow! Twin sons and a moose in the same year!" my brother Dick wrote to Vernon. Male children were highly prized in Newfoundland, and the twins were exceptionally happy there. I'd bundle them up when the mailboat blew its whistle, and we'd go down to the wharf, where the whole village gathered in excitement; or we'd stand on the porch and watch the men drive horses down the street outside our picket fence. The boys played hard every day and then, to our relief, slept so soundly that no noise could wake them.

Because they were our first children, we had few specific expectations about their behavior, which, in fact, seemed perfectly normal. They made all the sounds that are typical of babyhood and were very responsive to us. Perhaps we did miss a slight clue in the way they often put their hands over their ears and made loud rhythmic sounds that they repeated tirelessly. Apparently their hands transmitted to their heads the vibrations that they could not hear. We laughed at them when they did this, and they laughed back. The other couple who shared the house with us found this trick so cute that when they had their first child the next year, they tried to get him to do the same thing. When he showed no interest, they thought perhaps he was abnormal.

Because they were our first children, we had few expectations about the twins' behavior, which, in fact, seemed perfectly normal.

17

When Craig and Carson were ten months old, Vernon's two years of alternate service had been completed, and we returned to live in the little brick house near his home in Pennsylvania. During the next year clues to the twins' deafness obviously increased, and in retrospect now I must face an old guilty question I have never quite been able to reason away: How could we not have detected that the boys were deaf until they were two and a half years old? Some psychologists say that the parents of a deaf child are already aware of the deafness, at least subliminally, by the time the child is six months old. Were Vernon and I trying to hide this realization from ourselves?

Undoubtedly this was part of our problem. In our defense, however, I would say first of all that to the untrained eye, particularly to new parents, deafness in a child is not always as obvious as one might expect. Craig and Carson were very bright and alert, quick to imitate and explore.

In early pictures the twins face the viewer boldly with their high, intelligent foreheads, great blue eyes, and mischievous grins.

"Oh, they were so full of life," says their Grandpa Glick, throwing up his hands at the memory of their childhood, "so full of life!" In early pictures they face the viewer boldly with their high, intelligent foreheads, great blue eyes, and mischievous grins, while their arms and legs are busy exploring bath water, the kitchen floor, or a birthday cake. We were charmed by them and so benumbed by their constant activity that we never thought of them as lacking in preception. If anything, they seemed overstimulated.

Although these were our first children, both Vernon and I came from large families in which children were a way of life. A host of relatives visited us that year when the boys were between the ages of one and two, but none of them ever suggested that anything was amiss. Among themselves, I discovered later, they did murmur that "something ... wasn't quite ... right." Still, they were unable to define their vague suspicions. The most obvious thing that made the boys seem "different" was their sheer noisiness, which seemed scant evidence of abnormality.

All of us were a little bewildered by the phenomenon of twins; we assumed that twins would be "different." When Vernon and I attended a twins picnic and asked other parents about Craig's and Carson's delay in talking, they just laughed: "Oh, that's the way twins are; they have their own language. They don't need to talk to anyone else."

We were happy to be reassured and chose to ignore the increasing number of clues that we should have noticed. I remember one scene in particular which was to be replayed hundreds of times in the years ahead: as the twins went down the lane together, I stood in the doorway and called to them as loudly as I could, but they never turned.

Then when they were almost two, the unthinkable finally came out into the open. Late one afternoon Grandma Glick and I were noisily preparing supper in the kitchen while the boys slept undisturbed in the bedroom nearby. "Do you think maybe they don't hear?" she asked.

The words went through me like a flash, but then I tightened my grip on the potatoes I was peeling and became sensible again. "Oh, I think they do. They seem so . . . alert, you know."

I relayed the question to Vernon. The next day, when the twins were sleeping, he went into their room and clapped his hands near the bed. They didn't respond. Later we tried it again. They did wake up. Further tests seemed inconclusive. So for days we debated. Didn't the twins seem to talk to each other, gesturing and jabbering intensely? Didn't they seem to call and respond to each other from different rooms? Didn't they look up when an airplane flew overhead?

We consulted our family doctor, who set the twins in the middle of his office, then sidled around behind them and clapped his hands. They turned around. "I wouldn't worry about it," he told us kindly. We left his office in gratitude.

One would like to think that this kind of misdiagnosis was only a part of medical history, before doctors were as sophisticated as they are now. Unfortunately it is still common today. A study in 1970 showed that only 50 percent of the cases of deafness were correctly diagnosed in the first year, 40 percent were identified between the ages of one and two, and 10 percent after the second year of life. One reason for this poor record, according to the researchers, was that "physicians and other professional personnel receive inadequate training in diagnosing deafness and in helping parents of handicapped children."

Dr. Hilda Schlesinger, a California psychiatrist who has worked with many deaf children and their parents, agrees. Her message to doctors is this: "If parents come to you and say, 'I think my child is deaf,' you should believe them. The child is probably deaf. Parents know." All too often, however, general practitioners soothe the parents' fears, and the child loses the special attention that is so crucial in early life. Not all doctors can be expected to become experts in audiology. Deafness is not among the most common afflictions—about one child in a thousand has a hearing impairment from birth. However, if practitioners only followed Dr. Schlesinger's simple rule of thumb—to take the suspicion of deafness seriously—this alone would benefit a large number of deaf children and their parents.

The basic scene that took place in our doctor's office 20 years ago, recurs with startling frequency in the many stories about deaf children that I have heard since that time. Behind the backs of many deaf children, it seems, are these figures of authority, clapping for attention, and the results of these "gross noise tests" are almost always ambiguous.

This scene illustrates all too clearly several crude misconceptions about deafness. Most people think of deafness as total, but of course it is not. There are different degrees of

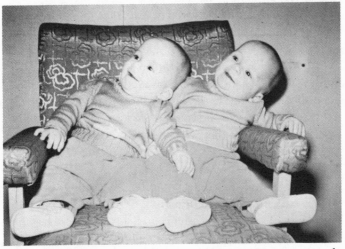

We were happy to be assured that the twins' hearing was normal.

hearing loss, so that a child might hear a loud clap but not the speaking voice. Deafness is also often selective, so that a child might hear sounds of one pitch but not another.

Those of us who have clapped behind the backs of deaf children have been simpleminded on another score as well. We the hearing think that a clap is a loud noise—but it is much more than that. A clap is also a sweeping movement of the hands, that casts subtle shadows and currents of air throughout a room. The deaf child lives precisely in this world of movement, light, and shadow, to which he is exquisitely tuned.

When Vernon and I first debated the possibility of hearing loss in the twins, we often told each other, "But when an airplane flies overhead, they look up. They can't be deaf."

"When you looked up," the boys told us years later, "we looked up too, to see what it was."

Recently I mentioned this revelation to our audiologist. He gave a tired, wry smile. "Almost all deaf children can hear or feel airplanes," he said.

In the fall of 1958 we moved to Canada again, this time to Calling Lake, Alberta. It was a mellow October day in Pennsylvania when, surrounded by relatives, we climbed into our overloaded Plymouth station wagon and pointed it northwest. As Grandma Glick waved goodbye under the huge shade tree beside the family farmhouse, I had the distinct feeling it was all she could do to keep from shaking her head in amazement that we were really undertaking such a foolhardy trip.

Our years in Newfoundland had given us a taste for adventure, and we had come home for a year only to gather our resources together for a more permanent move into the northland. For years Vernon and his brother Ike had dreamed of a pioneer life in Canada; Ike had already become a bush pilot in Calling Lake, and we wanted to join him and his wife, Millie, in that remote settlement of Cree Indians. There was just a touch of missionary spirit in our enterprise—we would attend a church in Calling Lake that was maintained by some 20 other American Mennonites—but we were not part of any specific church program and would have to provide for ourselves. Ike assured us that Vernon could find a job.

For a few days our excitement carried us north as fast as the Plymouth could pull its load of clothes, bedding, tools, canned food, and other possessions that were distributed in every corner of the car and packed tightly in a trailer behind us. While the soft air blew over us and the twins ricocheted against the half-turned-up windows, Vernon kept his eyes on the road, and I tried to stay calm. I was pregnant again.

We were glad to have the doctor's word that the boys were not deaf, but somehow we had to keep telling ourselves that they really were perfectly normal. On the way to Alberta we stopped to visit a friend who was an intern in a large city hospital, and we mentioned the story to him and his wife, hoping, I suppose, for further reassurance. His response was blunt and not a little cruel. "They're not right," he said, and then gave us a "professional" rundown of the possible diagnoses: maybe they were retarded, maybe deaf. I think he added, "No deaf people are smart," although perhaps my own fears exaggerated his actual words.

As we drove into Canada with this renewed chill in our hearts, the weather also turned rapidly colder until in Saskatchewan we barely made it through a snowstorm to a small town, where we were marooned in a motel room for several days. The prolonged confinement intensified the twins' hyperactivity to an almost unbearable pitch. Grimly we pushed on to Alberta and finally, at the end of the last 40 miles of frozen, rutted road, arrived in Calling Lake just as winter closed in behind us.

We stayed with Ike and Millie in their tiny cabin while Vernon looked for work, and I continued my losing battle to keep reins on the twins. In two weeks Vernon landed a job in the office of the local sawmill, and we moved into our own "house," a rough 24 x 24 foot shell divided into four equal rooms. There were no interior doors, no furniture, no stove, and no plumbing. The winter wind blew through an empty woodshed outside and worked its way easily through the sawdust insulation in our walls.

We moved in with a great sense of relief—at least the boys could run on their own territory again. We hung up blankets for doors, dug a stove out of the dump (it had been discarded by the local school board, so was hardly in mint condition), and found some water in a feeble spring behind the house. Now we had a home.

A month after we were settled in our drafty nest, a typical day went something like this: It was still dark when Vernon got out of bed and went to the kitchen to stoke up the fire. I could hear him break the ice in the large tub that held our water, now drawn from a hole in the lake a mile away since winter had frozen our little spring.

I waited as long as my sense of duty allowed, then put my own feet on the cold floor and struggled out to fix breakfast. We mumbled a few words around the stove, which doubled for both heating and cooking. Vernon brought in the day's ration of green firewood he had split the night before, and left for work.

With the first suggestion of light outside, Craig and Carson woke up and almost immediately began tearing through the house, dragging their separate but equally dirty security blankets behind them over the splintered floor. Within half an hour their yelling approached peak volume, where it would stay for the rest of the day. Bleary with morning sickness, I tried to reconcile my uneasy stomach to the coffee I so desperately needed, and thought with longing about the fenced backyard at our house back in Pennsylvania.

If the air warmed up to a relatively mild zero, we went for a walk (we could always use another trip to the outhouse anyway). Whenever I could get my hands on a stray arm or leg, I added another article of clothing to the boys' wriggling bodies, until the required number of layers had been reached. Often while I dressed one twin, the other took off his own clothes as fast as he could. Once, trying to evade me, Craig played the clown and fell backward into our open water supply. We used it anyway, of course.

When we got outside, the boys usually raced to some vehicle that had been jacked up for repairs, while I labored through the snow to make sure the blocks were securely fixed under the wheels. There was always some machine in our "yard" that had been immobilized by the cold. Starting

We chose to ignore the increasing number of clues of deafness that we should have noticed.

25

cars was one of Vernon's most frequent chores and the boys' favorite spectator sport. To start the car, he would first build a fire under the engine to heat it up; he would then run for the battery, install it with numb fingers, and try to get the engine turning before everything froze up again. Often the front wheels were also locked by the cold, and in any case the frozen tires always bumped solidly for the first five miles.

Craig and Carson, who knew every move in this game, swarmed over the car, playing mechanic with amazing accuracy until their hands were cold or I got tired of standing in the snow. Then we took a walk down the road, returning soon to avoid frostbite. In the afternoon, when cabin fever raged again, we repeated the expedition outside. As night came on early, I lit the kerosene lamp and tried to get some stew going on the stove. By the time Vernon came home, I was sick, crying over the stew that had turned into soup, while the twins bounced ever higher off the walls.

Small wonder that when someone at the mill said to Vernon, "It must be rough to have two kids crying when you get home," he replied, "No, it's when all three are crying that it gets me!"

Craig and Carson were two and a half, and we still couldn't talk *with* them, although we did talk constantly *to* them, and even read to them frequently. Like all deaf children, their "babbling" had been normal until they were about a year old, but after that time they had not developed the imitative sounds, including speech, that characterize the hearing child. Loud, incoherent, repetitious yelling had now become their common form of "expression." With a great deal of imagination, we would think they sometimes said "Mama" or "Daddy," and we kept telling ourselves how quick they were to imitate actions and how curious they were to investigate everything. But despair was beginning to pervade our drafty cabin. I cried, Vernon became more withdrawn, and the kids grew wilder and stuffed more security blanket into their mouths. In January the temperature rarely got above 30 below. It was the lowest time of my life.

This depression was not entirely without relief. The boys could be very affectionate, and at night, just before they went to bed, they climbed into Vernon's lap so that he could rock them to sleep. But even their habitually peaceful sleep now erupted sometimes into terror. Our moving had upset them, and they had become increasingly sensitive to any strange stimulus. We lived near a road on which trucks traveled at night, flashing rings of light and shadow around the walls of the room where the boys slept. Sometimes they would wake up and come running out, screaming, eyes wide as saucers.

In early spring Vernon took them finally on the long trip over bad roads to Edmonton to see two specialists in speech and hearing, who made a few perfunctory tests and then turned to Vernon. "You're the parents," they said abruptly. "You know they're deaf. Here's the address of a clinic in California. Maybe you can do something through correspondence. And bring them back when they're six."

Chapter 3

After Vernon and Ike and the twins bumped out of Calling Lake in the battered Plymouth that day, I went to bed in exhaustion. My pregnancy this time was attended by a host of complications, not the least of which were psychological. How, I kept thinking, could we bring another child into *this?* There was no answering my question; so that raw spring day I lapsed into a kind of stupor and slept as much as I could.

When the car rattled to a stop outside the house at night, I roused myself and lit the lamp. Ike carried in one sleeping boy and Vernon the other.

Vernon told me woodenly what the specialists had said. He is a man whose strong sense of commitment is joined by a great deal of emotional reserve, and that night neither of us knew what to say or how to console ourselves or each other. I'm not sure how I reacted. I went to bed and cried to myself, no doubt. That was so common in those days that it was scarcely memorable. But what I do remember from that night is the completely unfamiliar sound of crying that came from the other side of the blanket-door, where Vernon sat with his brother Ike in the kitchen.

It seems strange now that we should have been crying in separate rooms that night. Vernon, of course, felt that he had to be especially strong when I was sick in the latter months of pregnancy, and I am still grateful that he did carry so much weight physically and emotionally for all of us that winter. But I think the silence between us that night was all too indicative of our lives more generally. The twins were not the only people in our cabin with speech and hearing problems. They didn't have words to express themselves. We had words but were often unable to use them. We had very seldom talked to each other about the unusual behavior of the twins, although our fears for them had permeated our lives so completely, had become as familiar as our narrow walls, the broken stove, or the water we boiled and drank. We had been deeply disturbed by the boys' willfulness, by our inability to control them, and by the public disapproval of their behavior we had felt but never voiced. Nor had we

The twins at age 2.

29

confessed to each other our deeper feelings of guilt that we had somehow made a mistake in the way we were raising the twins.

The way Vernon and I reacted to deafness was influenced partly by the way we grew up ourselves. Both of us were raised in large Mennonite families in rural Pennsylvania communities, where our parents, the church, and finally God combined to form a structure that told us what to eat for breakfast, what clothes to wear, and what kind of Bible to take to church. My father was a schoolteacher-farmer, who controlled his one-room schools and his household more by the sheer presence of his unquestioned authority than by specific acts of discipline, and it amazes me now to recall that we eight children talked very little as we ate our meals around the long table. Papa never told us not to talk, but conversation from us wasn't expected. A small woman, who also brooked no nonsense, Mama had inexhaustible reserves of energy and devotion that were apparently available only to women of her generation. She did feel some frustration deeply, it seems, because she suffered from chronic insomnia. Often she crocheted all night while the rest of us were asleep.

Vernon came from an even more conservative family that belonged to an Amish church when he was young, in which the rules of conduct extended into such matters as what kind of fastener to use on one's clothes (zippers for a while were permitted but not buttons). His father, too, held almost absolute rule. Vernon knew at an early age that it was folly to argue openly against this situation, and learned to use silence as a final expression of any rebellion he felt.

On the positive side, our Mennonite background gave us a faith in God and His ultimate design that helped us to accept the twins' deafness. Oh, how we prayed! And the support we received from our families and our community over the years was beyond estimation. But the Mennonite way of life had also given us certain habits of repression that were less beneficial. We found it difficult to verbalize the fear and anger and frustration that we weren't supposed to feel. As the twins struggled for years to learn English, we too had to learn a language—of emotion—that we had never before expressed.

As the time approached for the birth of our new child, I became increasingly determined that this time it would take place in a properly equipped hospital. No more homemade incubators and pioneer heroics for me. My biggest worry was the 40 miles of mud road that separated us from the civilization of Athabasca, because in the spring this road could become an impassable quagmire.

When the pains began on April 25, 1959, we left the twins with a young girl, Pauline Beitzel, who had come up from Lancaster to help us, and started our long drive. The road was navigable, although the ruts were so deep that we had to stop the car whenever the pains seized me. We arrived at the hospital in time, in plenty of time as it turned out. I was in labor from 10:00 p.m. Saturday night until 1:00 p.m. Sunday afternoon, 15 hours in all. The long delay seemed almost an expression of my doubts about the life that awaited this child.

It was a girl. Kristine Joy, already "Tina." In spite of my apprehensions I was overjoyed. I had dreamed of having a daughter who would symbolize a change in our family life, a girl who would bring some feminine charm into our rough-cut world.

Tina did bring a new feeling of hope to us all. Craig and Carson clung to her bassinet and tried their best to play with her. When Vernon and I clapped our hands, jangled keys, and made noises over her bed, she turned immediately and smiled. She smiled at everything. And she could hear.

Even the earliest memory for both Craig and Carson, which dates from about this time, suggests a new direction in their lives. They remember almost exactly the same scene, although they don't recall discussing it with each other.

"I was walking in the forest with Craig and Pauline," says Carson. "It was dark because of the trees. There was a ball game going on, but Craig and I didn't want to be involved with that. We were restless. I remember the dirt road, with open space at the end, and right at the edge of the open space was the forest."

I'm afraid Vernon and I did not quite share this hopeful imagery of the road leading on into open space. A more accurate picture for us was the endless expanse of unmarked forest that stretched out below us when we went together on a plane flight into the bush. We knew that this forest could not give language to our boys.

We also knew that Craig and Carson were no longer the happy sprites they once had been. The pictures we have kept of our Alberta days are in marked contrast to the sunny Baie Verte slides. Only in one, a shot of Craig "changing a tire," does the old impish grin shine through, almost obscured by the dirt on the little mechanic's face and the frost on the camera lens. In another, more characteristic slide, both boys are standing on our rough back porch. The pose is defiant. Each child is looking down, in a different direction. The high foreheads are stubborn and the determined mouths shut tight.

So we began writing to deaf clinics and schools. The letters that came back to Calling Lake were sympathetic. Obviously the people involved in deaf education were dedicated to their work, because many of them replied with personal letters even though they had nothing to gain from us, and they offered us a surprising amount of hope. "It is evident that your boys have a great deal of hearing, since they say words," wrote an otologist from New York (I guess we had persuaded ourselves that those sounds really were "Mama" and "Daddy"). "The important thing is to get hearing aids on them. . . . We like to put two hearing aids on these babies . . . but if not two then one, and one at once and pay no attention to people who say that it cannot be done . . . then teach them at home as though they were normal children."

Almost every letter or school prospectus or article that some friend clipped and sent to us contained this word "normal." With the right kind of teaching, it seemed, deaf children could become almost like those who can hear. It would be a long time until we would read a very different kind of statement, in a book by a psychologist who has become one of our good friends. "When confronted with their child's deafness," says Dr. McCay Vernon, "the parents begin a process, which if successful will allow them to abandon the hope of having a perfect and normal child."*

But back at Calling Lake in 1959, we were eager to read more optimistic judgments than this. The one letter that carried most weight for us was from an acquaintance who was involved in speech and hearing rehabilitation himself. New methods of "oral" training, he said, were often so successful that "the only way of recognizing a rehabilitated deaf or hard-of-hearing person is by his hearing aid." Furthermore, he suggested, it was possible that the twins were not actually deaf; they might be *aphasic*. This would mean that they had difficulty retaining oral stimuli because of some injury in the right hemisphere of the brain.

Many children in deaf schools had been found to be aphasic, our friend wrote, and they needed the special train-

---

*McCay Vernon and Eugene D. Mindel, *They Grow in Silence: The Deaf Child and His Family* (Silver Spring, Md.: National Association of the Deaf, 1971).

ing that had been developed by the highly successful aphasic division at Central Institute for the Deaf in St. Louis. He sent a list of characteristics of aphasic, as opposed to deaf, children; and the aphasic column fit Craig and Carson with painful accuracy: they were "apprehensive," "not content to sit on mother's lap," "not interested in one thing very long," and "very noisy." If deaf children were more quiet and well-behaved and had longer attention spans, we didn't have any deaf children at our house.

But whatever the diagnosis, we were too far from all the clinics and schools that held the key to the twins' problem. By July we had decided to return to Lancaster so that we could get a clear diagnosis and start some kind of treatment and schooling.

We packed the Plymouth, now permanently crusted with the grime of Alberta, and left the black flies behind. Vernon and I sat in front; Tina was in a wooden box on the seat between us; Pauline sat in back; the boys were, as usual, everywhere.

When we reached the main road at Athabasca, Vernon and I looked warily at each other. This was the final deciding point in an argument we had been carrying on for the past several weeks. Vernon quite sensibly wanted to turn east and travel home as directly as possible; I wanted to turn west. Somehow through all that bleak winter I had kept a picture-postcard idea of Canada that I was determined to enjoy. I wanted to drive home through the Rocky Mountains; I wanted to see the parks.

We turned west. Vernon clenched his jaw and speeded up. First there was a smell of something hot, and then a screech that brought us to an abrupt stop. Vernon probed the bottom of the car and decided there was something wrong with the universal bearing he had just installed. We spent the night in town, had the car repaired, and resumed our trip—still westward through the parks, dragging our snowshoes in the trailer behind us.

Though obsessed now by the need to rescue the twins and ourselves from the terrible feeling that something was wrong, neither Vernon nor I was completely eager to go home again. Of course, I looked forward to living in a world of washing machines, electric stoves, grandmothers, and soft green lawns. But I didn't want to go back in failure. How could we face all the people who had admiringly seen us off on our big adventure? Most of all, how could we explain our long blindness to the fact that something was wrong with the twins? (Really, an internal voice kept asking me, how can you justify those two and a half years of negligence?)

I wish that Vernon and I had been able to discuss our apprehensions more openly with each other. Only now, so many years later, have I discovered that he, too, had mixed feelings about the boys and about our trip home. The loss of our pioneer dream was for him even more acute.

He felt at home in the northern wilderness. A highly disciplined man, he liked to test his wits in a harsh environment, liked to drive off in a jeep over the frozen snow for a hundred miles into places where there were no roads. It was a game for him to keep machinery going at the outer limits of its endurance. He learned to pilot a small plane and took long flights into the bush with his brother Ike. On their return they always flew low over our house, until the boys would tumble out to watch them land. Surely here in the north, Vernon felt, his sons would grow up to be self-reliant and strong.

Vernon came from a family of farmers and religious sectarians who believed that only through intense cultivation could the earth and the human spirit produce acceptable fruit. Never quite at peace in this environment, however, Vernon was drawn to the wilderness, where life was not

35

planted in rows. No longer the farmer, he became instead an avid hunter. He liked to stalk big game and, being a reticent man, enjoyed the laconic talk of hunters.

In the physical demands of the North, in its large expanses, he could begin to escape the cycles of repression, rebellion, and guilt that had constricted his youth. He was reluctant to return to his past, which still had a claim on him. It is no wonder then that when we discovered the twins' disability, Vernon was touched at first with the old harrow of guilt. As he recalls now: "I was so used to feeling it was my fault when things went wrong that I naturally thought I was somehow responsible for what was wrong with the boys." Their willfulness, even their inability to talk, seemed to repeat the stubborn silence with which he had met his own father's demands. This literal deafness seemed all too apt a punishment for his own youthful rebellion; and as always in the past, just at a time when Vernon had asserted himself, when he had tried to become independent, he was drawn inevitably back into the control of his family again.

Even now Vernon tends to regard his early feelings of guilt about the twins as peculiar to his own religious training. "Oh, I guess I thought I was being punished for wearing brown shoes—or for putting a radio in my car," he says wryly (these were some of the "sins" of his youth). "That's the way God was. You stepped over the line and he zapped you. And you never knew where the line was. He might change the rules in the middle of the game."

Books that describe the psychological problems surrounding deafness, however, say that guilt is a common reaction among parents, especially, as in our case, when the real cause of deafness is unknown. I wish we had been able to read some of those books when we were so bewildered and felt so alone, although actually the best books on deafness have been written only recently. I wish even more that

Vernon and I had been able to talk to each other about what was troubling us as we drove home with our heavy load in the summer of 1959.

Ironically, the reticence between us seemed to fuel our need to explain our situation to other people when we got back home. I talked endlessly about the boys to friends and relatives, half hoping for sympathy and advice, half trying to forestall it by showing that we really were doing everything we could.

Contrary to our fears, we found a sympathetic audience indeed, most notably in the members of our own families. Vernon's parents again provided a place for us to live—a small, blue tenant house behind the barn. We stayed there for a year while we began to search for an accurate diagnosis.

"I don't remember being particularly frustrated or angry at that time," Craig says.

"I think my childhood was happy," Carson agrees.

The twins enjoyed helping on Grandpa Glick's farm near Lancaster, Pennsylvania.

37

They remember riding the tractor over the tomato fields with their grandfather, and then watching the ripe fruit pour through the processing machinery that separated out the seeds for sale. They recall playing croquet and chasing the chickens through the barn in a big cloud of dust. I remember them waddling down the lane, imitating the ducks.

We always had a new story to tell about their antics. There was the time, for example, when they quietly closed our bedroom door while we were asleep, and then took flour and water to make pie dough in their room, gleefully smashing the paste into the sofa with a rolling pin.

They, of course, had no concept that they were different from anyone else—it was other people who were strange. They remember their distrust of the migrant workers, "the funny dark people" who lived in the barn. And they shied away from one of our friends because he had "a big mouth." He talked loudly because he was hard of hearing in one ear.

I'm not quite sure why Craig and Carson have so little recollection of the frustration which seemed to us as their parents so acute at that time. Perhaps in part they have repressed the unpleasantness, and in part we exaggerate it because of the great desperation we felt. Deep within us was the fear that their good spirits and intelligence might be wasted. On the surface we were almost constantly preoccupied with problems of discipline. For the next several years, as we groped toward a diagnosis and method of teaching the twins, we lived through what our audiologist says is a period of "pure hell" for many families with deaf children.

Craig and Carson, like 90 percent of all deaf children, lived in a very confusing situation. We, their parents, could hear, knew almost nothing about deafness, and had no contact with deaf adults. We could do little more than crudely modify the methods of child rearing that we had expected to use on a "normal" child.

Chapter 4

W hen the boys were three, I took them to Virginia for a visit with my sister Ellen and her two young boys. One afternoon there, when the combined energies of our four preschoolers had reached the threshhold of nuclear explosion, we decided they should all go outside. The winter day was unusually mild.

I put Carson's snowsuit on quickly; he began to yell as I turned to Craig, who threw himself on the floor in a fit of protest. Apparently Carson thought it was too warm outside to warrant his wearing heavy winter clothes, although he could not tell me this verbally.

My attempts at persuasion only made him more violent. It was in fact warm enough for him to go out with just a sweater on, and if I had been able to talk to him, I would have explained that, yes, today I could make an exception. But without that crucial explanation I knew that my leniency this time would only make Operation Snowsuit more difficult in the future.

At any rate, Craig's tantrum had already involved me in a

contest of wills that I could scarcely afford to lose. So I continued to insist, Craig continued to scream, and he had to stay inside that afternoon, making life miserable for all of us.

From the time the twins were two until they were five, this kind of scene recurred almost daily in our family. We explained, over and over, what we expected of them, gesturing and acting out the words; when we felt they willfully disobeyed us, as happened fairly often, we spanked them and made them sit in chairs and resorted to all the other traditional methods of discipline. This was somewhat therapeutic for us (I'm not sure how much good it did them). But always I was disturbed by the feeling that I was punishing someone who didn't really understand. And when I tried to cuddle them, to express my troubled love, they would squirm out of my arms, denying me even that solace.

I'm sure it looked to other people as though we were beating them sometimes. Their hyperactivity was so extreme that it often took a serious physical effort to deal with them. Tina remembers, from a later period, an oft-repeated scene I would rather forget: we often had to chase them through the house and catch them before we could administer punishment.

I don't mean to picture the twins' behavior as completely wild and erratic, however. The problem was often an inevitable result of the poor communication between us. A story I heard recently from another father of a deaf child illustrates this point quite clearly.

Bud was scheduled to pick up his son Mike and another deaf boy, Tom, at their school in Philadelphia, to bring them home to Lancaster for the weekend. On this particular Friday afternoon there was a terrible snowstorm, but since Bud knew how much the seven-year-old boys depended on his arrival, he loaded the car with ashes and shovels and set out.

On the way home with the boys, discovering that the turn-pike—their usual route—was closed, he turned off onto a side road to look for an alternative.

Immediately Tom went berserk, hit Bud in the face, pulled his hair, and screamed. He was afraid Bud was not going to take him home. Bud could not explain the deviation to him. The child became so violent that Bud finally had to stop, call the boy's home, and wait until his father drove through the snowstorm to reassure him. When the father arrived, even he could not explain the circumstances to his son, but at least the boy knew that, whatever happened, his father would now be with him.

This episode shows how dangerously simplistic it is to view the socialization and education of a deaf child as just a process of taming his wild impulses, as though he were an animal that had to be broken into obedience. The boy who screamed and tore at Bud's hair was not being willful. He was afraid. More than a "normal" child has, he had a desperate need to predict the details of his life, because deviations in routine could not be explained and thus were often frightening.

Craig and Carson also were very dependent on a regular daily schedule. They were actually most violent when their usual patterns of behavior were interrupted. Although we didn't see it quite clearly at the time, the deepest problem was ironically that their behavior might become too rigid, that they might become incapable of dealing independently with new situations in their lives. Their ability to change could grow only out of a dialogue with the rest of the world. Unfortunately, because communication among all of was so limited, Vernon and I sometimes met the boys' egocentric demands with our own inflexible ideas about how the world should be ordered.

Vernon and I were always in basic agreement in our

concern for the twins and in our choice of education for them. We were both deeply involved in the boys' daily lives and were ready to make sacrifices for them. Vernon certainly did not, like some fathers, reject his deaf sons or shove them into my lap—I'll never forget one mother who told me that her husband resented having to get off the freeway each morning to take his deaf son to school.

But Vernon and I did not fully agree on discipline, and this became a source of ill will between us at times. Although our differences were not great, the problems of deafness aggravated what might otherwise have been a minor irritation. Vernon worked into the night selling stereo equipment and tape recorders at a small business his father started. Somewhat stoic by nature, Vernon wasted no time in regretful dreams about the life he had left behind in Alberta. He threw himself into expanding the audio business, driven by the knowledge that we needed a great deal of money for specialists' fees and education.

Meanwhile, I had to live with the boundless energies of the twins almost without relief. And although Vernon helped take care of the children when he was home, I felt he expected me to rule them with a stricter hand than was possible under the circumstances. He, on the other hand, felt that I depended on him to pick up the psychological pieces of the family at night when he came home tired and that I looked to him to administer the necessary discipline!

Our early family life certainly did have an inescapable measure of anxiety. Even if Vernon and I had been models of empathy, we and the boys would often have been frustrated. In retrospect, however, I can think of two things that may have eased the tension between Vernon and me. One may seem rather facile: I wish that we would have taken time off to be alone, to escape the pressures of the household and get in touch with each other again. The other is more basic: I wish that somehow we could have assumed we were both doing our best in an inevitably difficult situation.

It is not easy, of course, to absolve yourself of guilt and doubt when the lives of your children are at stake. The question "Were we too strict?" still has a nagging persistence for both Vernon and me.

"When they were very young," Vernon says, "I punished them sometimes for things that—I realized later—they really didn't understand. That tears me up even now. I've talked to the boys about this, and they seem to accept my apology."

Another notable mistake we made was prompted by the mixture of religious concern and social pressure that so formed our lives. For years we tried to make the boys sit quietly through church services—attendance at church being a firm test among Mennonites of the required obedience to parents, community, and God. But Craig and Carson made loud incoherent noises and climbed over the benches, making every service for us more a problem of military control than a period of worship; we were forced to retreat to the basement long before the benedictory prayer. Since we knew the boys didn't understand speech, this seemed an empty exercise anyway. To make them sit through an hour-long sermon was almost a mockery of the biblical premise that "in the beginning was the Word."

Even more painful to remember is the debate we had for a while over whether or not to slap the boys' mouths when they made their loud noises in public. Fortunately our common sense won out over our fear of social criticism, and we never resorted to this punishment, which a child psychiatrist told us later would certainly have done the boys serious psychological damage.

There were many times when restraint was genuinely

43

necessary. The twins were often destructive and even endangered their lives. When we cleaned our basement furnace, which was situated under an open register in the floor above, we discovered a litter of burnt matches that they had struck and thrown below—and we had never even seen them doing that.

Craig and Carson say they do not harbor any grievances against our discipline in the early years, and it seems not to have left any deep scars on their personalities. I think there was a serious danger that we could have broken their spirits or crippled them with frustration, and I am thankful that the human psyche is often tougher than we might expect. It should be remembered also that their combined wills gave them a strength not accessible to the single, isolated deaf child.

When the boys were three, we knew few people we could consult who had previous experience with deaf children. Now we have many friends within the deaf community, and their perspective on some things is refreshing. When I recently asked a divinity student who is hard of hearing what he had observed about the discipline of deaf children by hearing parents, his response surprised me. I expected him, an energetic proponent of the rights of deaf people, to say that this discipline is often too harsh. Instead, he smiled and said, "Deaf children are great actors, great cons. They know how to get what they want, often by using deafness to their advantage."

He went on to say what I have heard from psychologists also, that hearing parents often vacillate in their treatment of deaf children, first punishing them in blind exasperation and then, smitten with guilt, becoming overpermissive and overprotective. Deaf children suffer from this confusion of emotions and learn sometimes to manipulate their parents' uncertainty.

44

on "galvanic skin response audiometry," in which the subject is administered a series of mild electrical shocks. A response pattern is first set up by repeating a loud sound which the subject can obviously hear, followed by a shock. After this, when he hears a similar sound without a shock, the subject will make a measurable physical response. This test is used on young children especially, because they cannot be counted on to give a voluntary signal when they hear a sound.

I'm sure the shocks were harmless, but as we saw the twins being wired up for the test, and then as we waited in the corridor with Craig's screams echoing around us, we couldn't help but feel a twinge of pain in our own nervous systems.

In Pittsburgh we also had our first view through the one-way windows that would become so familiar a part of later tests. As we watched our sons fumble with the blocks of an intelligence test, our own hands twitched, and we started

Craig with Mildred A. McGinnis ("Ginty"), founder of the Association Method for the education of aphasic chidren.

thinking up excuses for them in case they scored poorly.

As was always the case when we visited a clinic, the long trip increased the twins' hyperactivity. This time Craig was sick, making his diagnosis even more problematical. In spite of the wide margin for error which both we and the professionals recognized, however, the results of these particular tests would stand uncontested for the next three years.

The audiograms suggested a moderate hearing loss for both Craig and Carson, although we did not know how to read the graphs and—I'm ashamed to admit—did not ask anyone to interpret them for us. The letter from Pittsburgh was hardly definitive either. "It is not possible for us to rule out the possibility of hearing impairment in either of the boys," it said. But the next sentence hastened to make a careful gesture in the direction of other professional opinion: "This is not to say that the people who have worked with the boys over a period of time do not feel that their hearing function is within normal limits."

The confusing double negative of this jargon was just about as clear as our own view of the situation. By now we had been thoroughly shorn of our hope that the specialists were omniscient and could tell us exactly what needed to be done. We realized it was up to us not only to decide what kind of education to choose for our sons, but, even more frightening, it almost seemed we had to decide what really was wrong with them. We had to act and did not have the money to become like those parents who, as one professional describes them, "fly to California and back in search of some miracle cure." We still hoped that the boys' hearing loss was not too severe, and the tests seemed to permit that hope. We held onto the diagnosis of aphasia. Central Institute had a three-week parent-pupil program that I planned to attend with the twins in January.

We did seek some reassurance from the speech therapist

at the local hearing center, and got it—I guess. She stood up, closed the door, and then told us in a lowered voice, "Don't quote me, but I think you're doing the right thing." We didn't know whether to be pleased by her support or disturbed by her paranoia. There was some dispute between the hearing center and Central Institute which we never really understood, but apparently within the profession it was worth your job to keep such differences straight.

Meanwhile, following the advice of Dr. Kleffner and others, we decided to enroll the boys in a nursery school for "normal" children so that they would learn some general social habits and school routine. The psychologist-headmistress of a local school was glad to have them, in fact was eager to show *her* ability to manage their stubbornness. "Oh, this is just a case of delayed speech," she said to us condescendingly. "They're just tied to their mother's apron strings." I bit my tongue.

The school was in a staid old brick building, surrounded-ed by a high wall in a very respectable part of town. When we left the boys there the first day, they cried desperately, and as always there was no explaining to them what it was all about or that we would return soon to get them. We had to tear ourselves free under the skeptical eye of the headmistress, with the sinking feeling that maybe we were giving them more trauma than education. By the time we stopped outside the walls to listen, however, the screams had already subsided.

In the following days school became an accepted part of our routine; the boys seemed to get along well with the other children and even learned to lie more or less quietly on their cots during nap time. The headmistress must have felt that her criticism of us was justified. I don't know whether she noticed that when the boys left her school they still could not talk.

Carson's one memory of the nursery school sounds strangely haunting to me; he seems to have been almost on the verge of some new self-realization: "I remember seeing the kids when we were supposed to be taking a nap. I raised my head and was looking at—staring at—each kid alone, individually. It took me quite a while. I looked at how they slept, what kind of blankets they had, what toys they were closer to, and who was closer to—or farther away from—the window. I don't know why I was thinking that kind of thing, but I was. It took me quite a while, and eventually I got tired and went back to sleep."

Many people seem to think that deaf children live in a world that is empty and meaningless because it is not explained in terms of language, but Craig's and Carson's early behavior and their memories of those prelingual years show a surprising degree of comprehension. Images of light and shadow, of open and closed spaces, occur with such frequency in these memories that the temptation to read them symbolically is almost irresistible. Both boys remember especially our trip to Central Institute in St. Louis the next winter, in January 1961.

Carson recalls stopping in the night at an isolated motel, whose orange neon light was in sharp contrast to the surrounding darkness. Inside the office "a counter was on my left as I came in, and I looked up at a shelf and saw a bottle of orange soda pop. A big man was with us [Paul Rudy], and I began to beg for the pop; but he refused it to me, and then we went back to the car."

"Did I have the pop?" he asks me now, a twenty-year-old carried away by the vivid sensations he felt at four. "I think I did have a pop eventually, because in the back of my mind I remember having something cool in my hand. Yeah, I must have got it," he dismisses his reverie with a wave of the hand. "I must have got it after begging and ranting and raving or whatever."

Craig remembers traveling through a storm at night in "a packed station wagon" on that same trip. "The lightning hypnotized me," he recalls. When we reached St. Louis, the pace of the city struck him immediately. "It was so fast, so bold; we jumped in a taxi and took off!" And he remembers the streetcars, which to his deaf ears were noisy.

In the school, Carson recalls walking through a dark hallway: "The doors had windows in them, with a lot of light coming through that attracted me. I peeked in." The other children at the school seemed vaguely disturbing to both Carson and Craig. Carson remembers, "I think the classes were noisy." And Craig was definitely upset by what he saw: "When I was in the dorm, we were going up a series of stairs and came up into a big room with boys running around in their undershorts; some had nothing on. The TV was blaring. What surprised me most were the ladies [the housemothers] in the same room with these guys in undershorts. It was a kind of dark room, and the TV was such a bright white. Paul was saying something about the possibility that we could go to school and live there, but we didn't like it. I didn't want to be there."

Here Craig may, of course, be interjecting something he understood later; still, from what I remember of the boys' perception at the age of four, I consider it quite likely they did somehow comprehend that we were thinking of leaving them at the school. After our visits to other schools we had sometimes left the boys there alone, and they could assume that this pattern might be repeated again.

We communicated a great deal with informal gestures, and we knew each other's habits very well—but much of the boys' perception seemed to come from themselves. They had their own visual and emotional language, which seems

55

to have predominated internally for them until much later. "Even after we learned language, it was the picture of an object that came to our minds first," Craig says.

Neither twin remembers his first words, and only Craig remembers any scenes at all from the intensive tutoring they received at the Institute. "The teacher was holding up pictures of objects," Craig says, "and I was to name them or whatever. I came to one object and I couldn't think of it and the teacher was kinda getting mad. I was so upset, I was so frustrated I started to cry and the teacher took me out and we went down a long empty hall to a tiny room and she made me sit down at a desk and put a card in front of me: 'Come, tell me what it is.' You came in to check on me and I was bawling about it and you were giving me hints about what the word was. Then suddenly it hit my mind what it was, like a baseball bat hitting the back of my head: 'Knife!' "

For the three weeks in St. Louis the boys and I lived in a poor section of town in an almost empty apartment that Paul and Eva Rudy had rented but had not yet occupied. The walls were black with soot, and I had a terrible time trying to keep the boys clean as they ran, yelling, through the several rooms that were connected in circular fashion. "I remember the ceilings were very high," Carson says, "and as we ran around, we kept thinking we would get outside, but we always got back to the first room again."

Since we didn't have much money, we were grateful to the Rudys for giving us this place to stay. But everything seemed to go wrong. Someone tried to break into the apartment one night, increasing my apprehensions about the neighborhood. Another night, when Paul and Eva took the boys home to their trailer to give me some relief, one of the twins propelled a rocking chair so vigorously that he knocked out a plate-glass window. Even the TV the Rudys loaned us blew its tube. And finally, busy with his own responsibilities at home, Vernon forgot my birthday. "Nobody cares about me!" I lamented to myself. I broke into tears more than once; as always, the boys drowned out my sounds of desperation with their own noisy energy.

No trip into the outside world was casual; we always had a strategy, knowing that danger was always imminent. One day we went shopping downtown with Eva, planning that she would watch Carson and I would watch Craig. We were wandering through a large department store when suddenly Eva rushed up to me, her face pale. "Carson is gone," she gasped.

In panic we searched several floors, aware now of a peculiar silence in the bustle of the place. The yelling and noise that usually told us where to find the boys, was gone. For the next fifteen minutes I felt I couldn't breathe, caught in a nightmare I had always expected would come true—of my children lost in an uncomprehending world.

We approached a floor walker who obviously thought our anxiety was overdone. I found myself explaining rather incoherently something about aphasia. He directed us to the lost-and-found.

Meanwhile, Carson too had become frightened. He had lost us near a display of toys, which, he recalls, fascinated him, "because it was in the shape of a tree, with stuffed animals hanging on it." When the spell of the toys broke and he realized he was alone, he wandered out to look for us on the street, where he watched a policeman directing traffic. Then he returned to the store. "The next scene I remember," he says, "I was sitting on a counter eating an ice-cream cone and playing with pennies. People were fussing over me. I was scared."

This time we all woke up to a happy ending. At the lost-and-found I swept up Carson, ice cream and all, into my arms. But the fear of separation had not been exorcised as we went on our way. Carson remembers that "someone held [his] hand very tightly as we went out to cross the street and waited for the light to change."

Chapter 6

June Schwankhaus, our teacher at Central Institute, was a no-nonsense woman, who kept the boys in their seats longer than anyone else had up to that time. She repeated the vowel sounds tirelessly in front of their watchful faces; she put their hands on her throat, then on theirs; she insisted that they imitate her. When they succeeded, her praise was extravagant; when they failed, she was implacable. In three weeks they knew the vowels.

At the same time, I was learning how to continue this instruction at home. The boys were reluctant at first to accept me in my new role of teacher, but when Miss Schwankhaus read them the law, they settled back in their chairs again and went through their paces.

Back home we got chairs and a chalk board to outfit a little classroom in the large farmhouse where we now lived, and I became teacher for about three hours every morning. To illustrate each noun, we cut out a picture from a magazine and mounted it on a poster with dashes at the bottom to represent the number of sounds involved. Then for a

59

whole day we would labor over the sounds that made up, for example, "cat." Later we would try to use the word as normally as possible in conversation, and this process became so much a part of our lives that we began to hear from Tina's playpen the piping echo of "c-a-t. cat" as well. She never did go through a stage of baby talk!

Coming home for supper was more enjoyable for Vernon now; we were all eager to present him with the new vocabulary. Meals were still hardly leisurely, however. We insisted that the twins name any foods for which they had words, so everything stopped until the fragments of "j-ui-ce" or "m-ea-t" had been laboriously produced.

In three months the boys, now four years old, learned the 50 nouns that Miss Schwankhaus had assigned us, and with some pride we returned to Central Institute in April for another two-week session.

This trip west began with another series of disasters. We drove the last day through a terrible ice storm that left a trail of accidents along the turnpike. Just before we arrived at the Institute, I dumped a chocolate milkshake in my lap. Our stay in St. Louis was more enjoyable this time, however. We lived in a hotel closer to the school, and the lessons progressed rapidly as the boys learned to put their nouns into simple sentences.

Several restaurant scenes stand out in my mind from that period. It is often said that deafness is a "hidden handicap," and this seemed to be acutely true for us, especially when we were on the stage of a public dining room. While the boys were not quite so unruly now, they still misbehaved enough to provoke whispers of disapproval around us, and I was not inclined to stand up and announce that they were asphasic. No one would have understood that anyway.

Once, after I had taken Craig out to give him a spanking and then returned to the hotel dining room, a middle-aged man next to us, who had followed the whole thing with great interest, asked loudly, "Which one is the meanest? . . . Do you know what I'd do if I had a boy like that?" He scowled at our table with a mock-sinister face. Craig stared back and then made an unmistakable gesture, circling his head with his forefinger and pointing straight into the busybody's face. I shared Craig's sentiment exactly! "One for our side," I thought.

After returning home we continued our morning classes with more hope, although Vernon and I were troubled by the approaching decision of where to send the boys to school. Central Institute still couldn't guarantee admission in the fall. In any case we hesitated to send our five-year-olds so far away to such a large institution; the sight of those dormitory rooms had disturbed me as much as it had Craig. Then we heard that a new school, Pathway, was opening in the town of Narberth, Pennsylvania, near Philadelphia. Pathway School planned to have a special division for aphasic children.

Narberth was only 50 miles away, and in May 1961 we made a trip there to investigate. At the same time, McGinnis of Central Institute was planning to demonstrate her method to a group of specialists at a psychiatric institute in Philadelphia. She asked whether we would bring Craig and Carson to be her representative pupils. (See photo on page 51.)

People often ask what the world of the deaf child is really like. I don't pretend to know. But since Carson has a fairly clear recollection of Miss McGinnis's demonstration meeting in May 1961, I will try with his help to describe that scene from his point of view:

There were bright lights in Carson's face, and he couldn't see his mother and father, although he knew they were sitting somewhere in the group of people in the darker part of the room, where he could just make out the movement of heads and the occasional glint of eyeglasses. "Ginty" was writing on a portable chalkboard. Every line of her small figure—the stooped shoulders, the sharp face, the bright red lips—was familiar to Carson. She radiated a fierce kind of control that never relaxed. She was a familiar opponent, not quite an enemy but certainly not a friend; she was a force to be reckoned with. He slid off his portable steel chair and started toward the lights, but Ginty turned instantly and caught him before he had gone two steps. He had known this would happen. You couldn't get away from Ginty.

She set him back on his chair. He looked over at Craig, who was moving restlessly while sucking on a plastic toy. Now Ginty fixed Carson with that direct look that meant she expected a response. Her mouth moved in the rhythmic way that meant his name, and in the bright lights he could see how her tongue ended firmly on the roof of her mouth, and her lower lip drew down to expose an even row of teeth. She pointed at the first mark on the board, a "C," and repeated the movement that had started his name, but this time she stopped at the first sound. He could almost feel the strong rush of air that came out of her mouth and flooded her lower chin. He could do this too but didn't want to now. He wanted to be with his parents. He looked at the floor.

Ginty took a picture of a cat from another chair and knelt down so that the lights made her silver hair glow. Carson stared at the cat's open mouth, which was full of teeth even sharper than Ginty's. Out of the corner of his eye he could see that Craig was still sucking the toy. Carson shut his own mouth tightly and held onto his cold chair.

Nothing Ginty tried would change the fixed stares of the two boys, so finally she turned toward the other people and began to talk. Behind her erect back Carson looked at Craig. They both looked at the chalkboard.

"K-a-t," said Carson. "Cat."

"B-oa-t," said Craig. "Boat."

They began wrestling with the toy and slid off their chairs. "K-oa-t, coat." They read the whole list with glee.

While the audience in Philadelphia laughed at the twins' antics, one young audiologist said to his assistant, "Those kids aren't aphasic. Listen to that. Those kids are deaf!"

Several years later Pathway School sent Craig and Carson to this same Dr. Rosenberg, who remained their audiologist until his death. Only a few years ago, however, did I discover that he had attended the McGinnis meeting in 1961. "Most of us [professionals] came with a great deal of skepticism, which was confirmed when we heard the voices of those twins," he recalls. "Most deaf children have distinctive voices—and Craig and Carson were unmistakably deaf. Right then I could have drawn a close approximation of the audiogram which we eventually got."

The audiograms which Dr. Rosenberg did get for Craig and Carson three years later in 1964, the same audiograms which he still draws for them now, show clearly that both boys have a "profound hearing loss."

These audiograms show a much greater hearing loss than the Pittsburgh tests indicated in 1959, when the twins were four. Apparently those earlier tests, which strongly influenced the diagnosis of "aphasia," were inaccurate. Professionals who are acquainted with the twins now are almost unanimous in their opinion that Craig and Carson were always deaf and were not aphasic.

"There is no excuse for the kind of misdiagnosis the twins received in their early lives," Dr. Rosenberg said years later, "but it still happens frequently and sometimes the results are tragic." He had actually seen so many of these cases, that it became a kind of hobby for him to bring the problem to the attention of his colleagues.

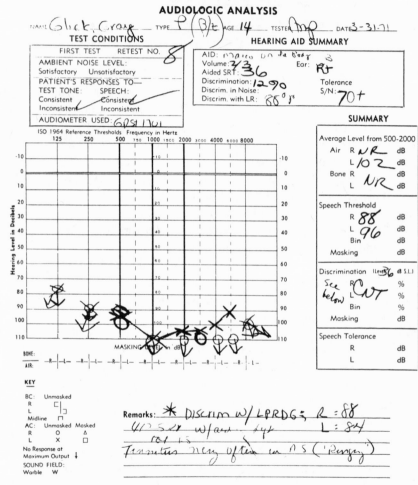

More recent audiograms, such as the 1971 analyses charted here, show much greater hearing loss than the Pittsburgh tests indicated

Section of Audiology Department of Otorhinology
TEMPLE UNIVERSITY HEALTH SCIENCES CENTER

Philadelphia, Pennsylvania 19140

AUDIOLOGIC ANALYSIS

NAME _GLICK, CARSON_ TYPE _Bd of Ed_ AGE _14_ TESTER _ML_ DATE _3-31-71_

TEST CONDITIONS	HEARING AID SUMMARY

FIRST TEST   RETEST NO

AMBIENT NOISE LEVEL:
Satisfactory ✔ Unsatisfactory
PATIENT'S RESPONSES TO—
TEST TONE: SPEECH:
Consistent   Consistent
Inconsistent   Inconsistent
AUDIOMETER USED: _MA24_

AID: _Maico BC_
Volume: _3-4_
Unaided SRT: _34 dB_   Ear: _Left_
Discrimination: Tolerance _75 dcbe_   _SAT 30 dB_
Discrim. in Noise: S/N:
Discrim. with LR: _2 vc_
at Vol 4 - Do Charge

ISO 1964 Reference Thresholds Frequency in Hertz
125 250 500 750 1000 1500 2000 3000 4000 6000 8000

Hearing Level in Decibels

MASKING LEVEL in dB

BONE: —R—|—L— —R—|—L— —R—|—L— —R—|—L— —R—|—L— —R—|—L— ·L—
AIR:

KEY

BC: Unmasked
R   ⊏
L   ⊐
Midline   ⊓
AC: Unmasked Masked
R   O   Δ
L   X   □
No Response at
Maximum Output ↓
SOUND FIELD:
Warble   W

Remarks:_____

SUMMARY

Average Level from 500-2000

Air   R _98_ dB
       L _95_ dB
Bone   R   dB
       L NR dB

Speech Threshold
       R _84_ dB
       L _88_ dB
       Bin   dB
Masking   dB

Discrimination (Level   dB S.L.)
       R   %
       L   %
       Bin   %
Masking   dB

Speech Tolerance
       R _100+_ dB
       L _100+_ dB

SAT R _76 dB_
     L _74 dB Hz_

10846

in 1959, when the twins were four. Misdiagnosis still happens, and sometimes the results are tragic.

65

Why then didn't he tell us back in 1961 that the boys had probably been misdiagnosed? "I was playing a waiting game. I didn't know of a better program for them to get into at the time," he explained.

It is difficult for me to accept the idea that we should have been kept partly ignorant of the uncertainty that surrounded our sons' disability 15 years ago. We thought we were asking a lot of questions then. We should have asked even more. If we *had* asked more questions in 1961, we may have discovered that in fact McGinnis's concept of aphasia in children was not as clear-cut as we assumed.

It was based really on an *apparent* similarity she claimed to see between soldiers in World War I who because of head injuries had lost their ability to speak and certain children at Central Institute who had difficulties with language that could not be explained fully by a diagnosis of retardation or hearing loss. This analogy makes quite a jump—from the obvious case of an adult with a head injury to the much less demonstrable case of a child with an unknown congenital disorder—but McGinnis was a fiery Irish lady with enough energy to make that leap and then go back to build a school that would bridge the gap.

"When she was right," recalls a former colleague, "she was very right; and when she was wrong, she was very wrong." McGinnis was not inclined, however, to admit the latter possibility. When I was at Central Institute, I saw what happened when one parent questioned some point of the method. Ginty took the heretic into another room, treating her to an extended harangue. The message came back clearly to me through the closed door. Any alteration of the method, it seemed, might damage a child's future irrevocably. When Ginty returned still sputtering her wrath, it was all that I, an innocent bystander, could do to keep my knees from knocking together.

As she grew older, McGinnis's following declined, and soon after her death the aphasic division at Central Institute was discontinued. The term "aphasia" is now most often used to describe the speech dysfunction that sometimes follows a stroke in adults; it is rarely applied to children. In all fairness it should be added that some professionals do still recognize a speech problem which is similar to McGinnis's definition of aphasia, even though they do not subscribe to her entire system. "Auditory imperception" and "central language disorder" are terms that are currently in use.

Of course, when we looked for a school, we were not so much interested in theory as we were in results, and there was no questioning the fact that the Association Method had given a measure of speech to Carson and Craig. Hence, it was a tremendous relief to us that Pathway School could continue the same method of instruction—if we could find the $4,000 for tuition and if we could find a place for the boys to live. The school had no dormitory facilities.

We enrolled the twins with no certain idea where the money would come from; our application for state aid proved fruitless. However, our families and community were watching this leap of faith (or naiveté). They made sure we landed on solid fiscal ground. At least a dozen members of our two families contributed a total of about $900, friends and acquaintances added another $350, and finally our church insurance company, Mennonite Aid, dipped into their catastrophe fund for $2,000. The balance was at least manageable for us.

Our church community helped us solve the additional problem of where Craig and Carson would live. Two Mennonite families in Frazer offered to become foster homes. Ralph and Erika Malin, who lived with their four children on a small farm, agreed to board Carson. Ernest and Wanda Swartz, who resided nearby, took Craig into their family of seven. Our visits to the two homes reassured us beyond a doubt that the boys would have a good life there.

One problem remained. How would the boys get to Narberth every day, 16 miles away?

A lurch of the train caught me just as I was reaching for Craig, and set me down rudely in my seat. Still climbing toward the open window to feel the hot, cindery air of late summer blow on his face, Craig laughed but then turned serious when he saw how determined I was.

"Sit down." He knew this command very well and slid back into the seat beside me. Carson, meanwhile, had his hands on the edge of another window and was watching the houses on main-line Philadelphia go by.

"Look," I said sternly, "if you put your hand out the window, another train might come by and knock it off." Of this warning, Craig and Carson knew only the words "hand," "train," and "off," but my gestures seemed to give them at least some idea of the disaster I predicted. The two boys turned to each other and began "talking in aphasic."

The conductor stopped next to us. "Fine pair of boys," he said.

"Say, do you make this trip at the same time every day?" I suddenly realized I was gesturing and pronouncing every word distinctly, as though I were still talking to the boys. "Could you see that these two get off every morning at Narberth? Starting tomorrow they'll be going to Pathway School."

"Excuse me," he said, and went away to punch a ticket.

"All right," he said on returning. "You want them to get off at Narberth. I'll see to that."

"And in the evening they'll go back to Paoli on the 3:45 train."

He repeated this information, while listening in puzzlement to the intense gibberish the boys were talking.

"They're aphasic," I explained, taking a breath. "That means . . . [I tried to decide whether to give him the long or short definition] they don't understand language very well. They. . . ." The conductor nodded sympathetically.

"I have some signs here," I said, bending over to fumble under the seat. At that moment the boys saw a dog in a backyard and leaned out the window for a better look. I reached for them with one hand and jerked the plastic-covered cardboard signs up with the other, snagging my nylons. On one side the signs said *Pathway School, Narberth, Pa.*, followed by a phone number; on the other side they said *In Care of Ralph Malin* and *In Care of Ernest Swartz*, with their respective numbers.

"The boys will wear these pinned to their backs," I told the conductor, who looked a little bemused. "In the morning *this* side will be out, and then in the evening someone at the school will pin the signs on so the *other* side shows."

I went on explaining how one woman would take the twins to the Paoli station and another woman would get them in Narberth and still another woman would pick them up in Paoli in the evening; I had a sinking feeling that this was all ridiculously complicated and I was a fool for ever thinking it would work. The conductor nodded and left. The train slowed and I read the Narberth sign as it flashed by.

"This is where you will get off," I said to the twins, checking in vain for some landmark to point out to them. These stations all looked alike, I thought, except for the next one— at 30th Street in the middle of Philadelphia; if these five-year-old boys forgot just once where to disembark, and no one reminded them, they would end up in the grimy heart of the city!

That evening after we had left Craig and Carson at their foster homes, we drove back to Lancaster in despair. How could Vernon and I have assumed that two aphasic boys would make all those connections, day after day? Surely this time we had risked too much.

We made some frantic phone calls that night to arrange that someone unknown to the boys would follow them on their first trip. Then, after little sleep, I alternately prayed and drank coffee until the phone rang the next evening.

"You won't believe this," said the woman who had shadowed the boys, "but they got on the train, went straight to their seats, and sat there quietly until it was time to get off!"

Chapter 7

Because Pathway School had no buildings of its own, it held classes in Narberth Presbyterian Church, an imposing stone structure that awed the twins when they entered it for the first time. Craig remembers that it looked like a "castle." Carson recalls being frightened in the dark lower halls by a powerful sound that must have been the organ.

Clutching tightly to my hands, the twins entered this mysterious world. "I had the feeling I was going into something new," Carson says. "We were led through doorways, through dark halls, and then suddenly we came out into a big room. The bottom half of the room was 'junky': there were portable dividers, movable chalkboards, tables, and chairs, but up above was . . . nothing. Just bare walls and a very high ceiling. I kept looking up there. I couldn't understand that."

The two main divisions of the school, one for children with minimal brain damage and one for those considered aphasic, sought partial privacy behind makeshift dividers in two rooms, which had to be cleared each weekend to make way for Sunday church services. An attempt was made to separate the students into small classes on the basis of their similarities. The range of disabilities was so great, however, that in each class there was a difficult mix of physical handicaps, hearing impairments, and behavioral problems.

"It was a zoo, educationally," recalls Lillian F. Wilson, former director.

Despite its awkward beginning the school always impressed me more by its structure than by any evidence of disorder. Much to its credit, Pathway did not try to conceal its daily operation from parents; quite to the contrary, the staff insisted that parents attend at least one session a week themselves.

With the help of Craig and Carson, I have tried to

Miss Carpenter ("Carpy"), left, instructing Craig and Carson in the early days of "sounding out" words.

recreate a typical classroom scene from their first year in Narberth. This was one of the most intense periods of our lives.

I sat behind the semicircle of small chairs that faced the chalkboard; this sparse furniture was the only stable reference point in the room. The five children were more or less within the orbit of their chairs, and the teacher was generally located near the chalkboard, but there was so much movement, so much shifting of energies among teacher and pupils, that my head often ached from trying to keep everything in focus.

"Teddy," the teacher, was determined to control this random energy. A young girl with long, straight black hair, she was thin and very fit, like a physical-education teacher. Her features were sharp and usually stern. She moved her pointer and spoke with great precision.

Her teaching goal for this day was deceptively simple. The children were supposed to learn to read the following exercise, written neatly in cursive script on the chalkboard:

b o-e t	b oa t	b ow t
b ee t	b ea t	b ea t
b oo t	b oo t	b oo t
b ae t	b ai t	b ay t

"Carson, please stand up!" Teddy's voice was loud; her pointer and the direction of her eyes gave Carson the real cues as to what was expected of him. He got up and toed a chalkline on the floor, putting him in a position where he could read the board, but his face would still be fully visible to the rest of the class. The pointer rested on "b ae t."

"B. . .a-e. . .t." Each letter produced a separate explosion of sound. The word meant nothing to Carson. He labored simply to move his mouth, expel air, and vibrate his throat in a way that would please Teddy and ensure him a certain status among the other children. The rest of the class fidgeted in their seats, watching to see whether he would make a mistake. The pointer moved to "b ai t."

"B...a-i...t." Then to "b ay t."

"B...a-e...t."

"Very good, Carson!" Teddy's smile left him proud and bashful. He dug an elbow into Craig when he returned to his seat. Craig pushed back. Teddy frowned and they subsided.

Chippy was next on the line. The other children sensed there was something "different" about Chippy and—although they liked him—often picked on him. He had a large head, whose size was accented by a crew cut and a long, jutting jawline. Beset by several tics, he had the strange habit of suddenly bending over double to touch the floor when he was nervous. His parents were deaf.

"B...o...," Chippy read.

"No, no!" Teddy shook her head. "B...a-e. B...a-e. Try it again."

While Chippy wrestled with this syllable, the other children began waving their arms for attention, some stood up, and there was a cacophony of sounds as they all tried to give the correct answer.

"Sit down!" Teddy's wrath was sudden. "Chippy is reading now." As the children dropped into their chairs, Craig almost went over backward. Having been agitated by Carson's success, and eager for attention, he twisted in his chair to look at me. I made a circling motion with my hand, which he reluctantly obeyed.

Teddy turned all her fierce concentration on Chippy, who was shifting uneasily at the chalkline, fighting the impulse to bob down and touch the floor for reassurance. "B," said

Teddy, pointing to the "b."

"B," said Chippy.

"Good. Now 'a-e,'" she said slowly, her mouth open wide.

"Eh," said Chippy.

"A-e."

"Eh."

Teddy repeated "a-e" again and again until at last, like a feeble spark, this fragment of sound or motion of the lips, or whatever it was to Chippy, jumped a gap somewhere in his head and returned through his awkward mouth again: "B. . .a-e, baet."

"Good!" Teddy beamed. It was as though an electric current ran between her and Chippy. He returned to his seat in a daze. The other children, free of Teddy's control for the past five minutes, were jiggling frantically on the edges of their seats.

Craig was next. In an effort to show off he slurred the

The twins with Chippy (center), a classmate friend at Pathway School, enjoy a break from their studies

sounds and had to repeat. He slurred again. Worse than that, he ignored Teddy for a moment and turned to make a face at Carson, who was clamoring to take his place.

Suffused with anger, Teddy instantly slapped Craig's arm. He turned immediately sullen, with tears in his eyes refused to say anything more, and finally retired in disgrace to his seat.

A helpless observer, I felt the sting of Craig's punishment as acutely as he did. I did not think it was fully deserved. I knew how much he wanted to please, knew the rivalry between him and Carson, who was a better student and received more praise. I had seen Carson taunting Craig after his first mistake.

At the same time, I could sympathize with Teddy's frustration. Above all, I did not want any motherly interference from me to jeopardize Craig's standing with his teacher. Like Craig, I accepted the blow in silence. When I talked to Teddy after class, I would not question this act of authority.

The lesson proceeded to Gail, a pretty little girl of seven, who always had her blonde hair set in curls and tied up with a bright ribbon. Gail was a flirt. While she read in her surprisingly deep, coarse voice, the boys all twisted in their chairs and nudged each other. When she sat down, someone pulled her curls.

Mike was the last. Fourteen years old, he towered above the other children. Mike had previously spent ten years in several schools for the deaf. Tests seemed to show that he had average intelligence, and some professionals even argued that his hearing was normal. Yet for some unknown reason he had never talked. He came to Pathway unable to say a single word.

As Mike stood up, the other children grew quiet, and Teddy seemed to stiffen visibly. Mike stood at the chalkline, with hands and face clenched as though he were facing his execution. Teddy pointed to "b ae t." Mike's lips moved, but no sound emerged.

"B. . .a-e. . .t," Teddy pronounced.

Mike's whole body struggled, and his mouth emitted a sound that was more a bleat than speech: "Bah."

"B. . .a-e. B. . .a-e. B. . .a-e."

"Bah."

Mike's face was contorted. It seemed that it was all he could do to keep from exploding, to keep from striking back at the teacher, the chalkboard, the pointer that demanded responses he could not give. But over the years Mike had learned a terrible self-control. Almost the size of a man, he stood and bleated and clenched his fists until finally, hoarse with frustration herself, Teddy lowered the tip of her pointer in defeat and let him return to his seat.

She turned and wrote a final, single word at the bottom of the exercise: "boat." With a tired smile she taped a bright picture of a sailboat on the board. After two days of laborious "cross-drilling" from "b. . .o-e. . .t" to "b. . .ay. . .t," the class was ready to learn a new word.

In its first year there was a decided sternness about Pathway School. Craig and Carson remember being "terrified" of several teachers. Punishment was swift and sometimes harsh. One day, when Craig climbed up a wall divider to see what the class on the other side was doing, the teacher responded with a well-aimed eraser that bounced off his nose and caused it to bleed copiously.

More disturbing was one episode involving Mike. "The rest of us understood what the teacher wanted, but Mike couldn't or wouldn't, do what she said," Craig recalls. "She got so mad finally, she threatened to spank him, and then she went over to the window and either threatened to throw him out or told him to jump out himself. He started to cry and then I started to cry and soon the whole class broke down and cried." For days afterward the children "talked" about this among themselves with great gesturing, and even opened the window to debate whether they would be able to make the frightening jump.

This episode certainly shows a lack of control on the part of the teacher which cannot be condoned. Still, I think many parents of deaf children would understand, if not approve of, the frustration that the teacher felt.

Mike's own mother deeply appreciated this same teacher's desperate attempts to wrest speech from her son. "I remember how she struggled with him," she says. "I remember her with her hand in his mouth, twisting his tongue to try to get him to talk. In two weeks he said his first words, 'mother' and 'father.' I broke down crying when I heard."

Seeing Mike's tragedy, I realized how much our family had to be thankful for. Craig and Carson were still young enough to learn, and the teaching seemed to connect with them. Progress was slow, to be sure. The first year they worked mainly on nouns. It was two years before they used past tenses of verbs. Only in the third year did they tackle the difficulties of the pronouns "he" and "she." But over the period of a semester we could see a marked improvement in their speech, and we were grateful.

I certainly do not mean to imply that Pathway was a place where children were tortured with the "instruments" of speech. There was often laughter in the classrooms. The children soon found that language had some value to them. For example, the class went to a restaurant one day, where each child ordered his own lunch: "I want... a ... hambur-ger ... and ... a ... C-oe-k." (I'm sure the waitress had no idea how many hours of labor went into that simple request!) The children also were encouraged to express their emotions, and "I ... am ... angry" became a familiar refrain at home and at school. 78

Some teachers tried to meet the needs of the children honestly, even if this meant forgetting about the Method for a day. In a later year, when several children in one class raised questions about sex (one boy, for example, thought he was making babies every time he went to the bathroom), Lois, the teacher, gave them the basic information they needed. She felt quite rightly that the parents of these children were especially reluctant to talk about sex. One has to be fairly explicit about this when talking to a deaf child; a vocabulary of only 500 words affords little subtlety.

The children could scarcely master the polysyllables of their teachers' names, so these were shortened (Theodora became "Teddy," Miss Carpenter became "Carpy"). The nicknames added a nice touch of informality to the school. In general, the atmosphere was more relaxed after the first year. The twins developed a great attachment to some of their teachers, notably Lois and Carpy. They will always remember the day Carpy invited them to her apartment for dinner, treating them to their first look at cartoons on TV.

Chapter 8

By the time I took the train with them later that year, the twins had become seasoned little commuters. They boarded the train ahead of me and went right to their accustomed seats through a hail of greetings from their fellow passengers. The woman behind us introduced herself, explaining that she always sat there to keep an eye on them.

"Now watch this," she said as the train made its first stop. The twins hurried up the aisle and ushered each passenger to his seat, collecting a toll of candy wherever they could. Then if anyone pulled out a cigar or cigarette, they darted to his elbow and worked the lighter for him.

The woman behind us, who would go down in the boys' memory as "the lady with the green gum," reassured me that Craig and Carson were usually well-behaved. "Oh, sometimes they have a dispute, and the books and lunchboxes fly, but someone always restores order," she said.

Before the train had even slowed for the Narberth station, the boys were ready to get off. As soon as the doors opened, they rushed onto the platform, went straight to the newsstand, waved perfunctorily to the lady there—and then began stuffing their pockets with candy and bubble gum. This is what I had been waiting for. "No!" I reprimanded them. "We didn't pay for that!"

The woman behind the magazines smiled. "Oh, it's all right. I let them take whatever they want. They're both so cute."

"We appreciate your generosity," I said, "but the teachers at the school say that the boys come in and pass the candy around every morning, and it disrupts the class. And I don't want them to get into the habit of just picking up things without paying for them."

Like many people, this woman was taken by the boys' alert appearance, pitied them because of their handicap, and let them do whatever they pleased. It was not a pattern I wanted reinforced. After a long talk the woman agreed to give the boys candy only when they brought nickels along to pay for it.

In a few weeks it became apparent, however, that the boys' infrequent nickels now "bought" them anything they wanted at the newsstand, so I made another trip to the station and went to the root of the matter, where I should have started. "Look," I explained to the boys, "do not take any candy. It does not belong to you."

The next day, according to the woman who met them at the station, one boy started to grab candy as usual, but the other shook his head, seized the offender's hand, and hauled him off to school.

By the middle of their first school year, the twins' behavior had changed markedly. At the age of five they were no longer the wild animals they once had seemed to be, howling, as one professional now puts it indelicately, "like Siamese cats in heat." Their new ability to communicate, in however laborious a fashion, had helped to channel their energies, and the highly structured teaching had begun to have some effect.

Now they were great sticklers for certain kinds of order. One morning when the boys met on their way to school, Craig became upset, pointed, gestured, and "swore in aphasia" as we used to say. The cause of his intense irritation was soon apparent. Carson's foster mother had put the "wrong" pair of pants on him that morning, so the twins were not dressed in their usual matching outfits.

In general, the boys hated any change in their schedule. Another day, when the woman who usually picked them up at the Paoli station forgot them and arrived in panic an hour late, both boys got up from their seat on the steps and gave her a dressing down in their private language which fully expressed their outrage at her absentmindedness.

A psychologist-friend of ours points out that the twins' increasing insistence on routine and their conformity to the demands of authority were perhaps a mixed blessing. "This

The twins and Tina enjoyed their visits with Grandma Pellman.

is the kind of rigidity the McGinnis Method caused," he says. It was certainly fortunate that Craig and Carson could escape the rigors of their school and go back in the evening to the freedom and warm family life they enjoyed in their foster homes.

Craig remembers playing with the Swartz children on their wide lawns, after which he was served good country meals by "Mom" Swartz, who was "gentle, helpful, loving—like the whole family was." Carson says of the Malins, "They were kinda happy, very family-oriented. I had a lot of affection for Erika [Mrs. Malin]. She was a very motherly person and a good cook."

Carson's free-association memories of the Malin farm sound almost like the dream of a perfect childhood: "I remember the chickens, the sheep, the meadows, trees, the rabbits, the orchard, and the muddy swimming hole in the valley behind the house at the end of a trail the sheep had made. I remember the men shearing the sheep, and walking

Tina and her brother took good care of Grandma's kitten.

up the hill to church. I went into the chicken coop and got pecked. There was a large garden, too. They had a large, messy basement, where I would roller-skate on rainy days. Mr. Malin had a den, a study with many shelves, where I could find exotic books. I remember how I learned to eat asparagus and how I was spanked for not eating it. I remember meeting Craig in the car on the way to school, and how I was injured falling off the porch. And I remember seeing the clouds on fire [at sunset], looking up at the sky."

Mrs. Malin recalls that both twins had an air of independence about them: "They were their own men right from the start." And although she remembers that at first they were apt to assert themselves by "screeching," later in the year Carson began to talk more and paraded around the house, endlessly repeating the syllables of a new word like "spaghetti." He tumbled with the Malin children on the liv-

Craig and Carson with three of the Mennonite Voluntary Service houseparents who provided a home for fourteen "aphasic" children a block away from Pathway School.

ing-room floor but, like any member of a large family, learned how to scheme to get his privacy. Jimmy Malin remembers that the twins used to lock themselves in the bathroom and read comic books. They seemed to enjoy the quietude of their deafness while the rest of the family clamored at the door.

There was an established order in these households which Vernon and I and the boys trusted fully. Ralph Malin was a minister, and the Swartzes were also deeply religious. Craig remembers how hard it was for him to wait with food on the table while Mr. Swartz read the Bible and prayed! Still, neither family demanded more attention to religious matters than the boys were able to manage.

Living in separate homes gave the twins a much needed opportunity to assert their individuality. Up to this point in the story I have spoken of them as though they were one person with four arms and two heads, but this was definitely not the case. By the time they started at Pathway their early differences had taken such distinct form that the director there could typify Carson as a child who was more interested in people, and Craig as a person more interested in "things." They were still so identical in appearance that their teacher finally demanded they wear different-colored shoes to school. Soon, however, their performances in the classroom set them apart.

Carson was more of a scholar and more verbal; he liked to be "teacher" and was a leader on the playground. At times he was inclined to be a little rebellious, especially if he thought he or some other child was being treated unjustly. If the class didn't move fast enough to suit him, he knew how to act bored.

Although he was a good student too, Craig was less able to concentrate on academics. As one teacher remembers, "he was more interested in playing ball or looking for frogs."

His pronunciation was more slurred, and he was apt to forget what he was saying in the middle of a speech exercise. Craig was adventuresome but often depended on Carson to set the pace for him.

Although they were united against the rest of the world, the boys often quarreled between themselves. "On the train," Craig recalls, "I used to turn the seat so I could keep away from Carson." And in times of crisis they were both apt to say, pointing at each other, "Get rid of him!" This rivalry became increasingly acute with age.

The second year at Pathway, 1962-63, Craig and Carson lived with twelve other "aphasic" children in a large old house just a block from the school. Now they could rush "home" for cookies and milk in the afternoon and then go out to play in the park. The twins joined up with Pat and Tom, two older boys, to form "the big four." Generally all the children in the house became good friends.

Friendship included plenty of rough-and-tumble activity, but in this "cozy" house, as Craig remembers it, the number of children was small, and supervision was close enough to give each child the attention he needed. There was little of the bullying that can make life miserable for children in some larger residential schools, or make it almost impossible for a deaf child in many public schools for hearing children.

The noise level in the house could reach Babel proportions that made it difficult for a hearing adult to imagine the near-silence in which some of the children lived. The houseparents soon learned, however, to communicate within the limits of the "aphasic" world, and made do with gestures when speech failed. Rubbing their hands together and pointing upstairs meant time to wash. The children too developed a small vocabulary of gestures to supplement their laborious English. If they wanted to say that they liked someone, they would hold two fingers together to indicate

86

how close they felt. To show dislike they eloquently shielded their eyes and looked away.

The four young houseparents, who had been placed at Pathway by the Voluntary Service organization of the Mennonite Church, received only room and board and $10-a-month spending money for their work. Motivated by their desire to help the children, they put extra effort into the job. There were weekly trips to the bowling alley and skating rink, and games at home such as a play store, where the children could practice buying things. Part of a tradition of discipline themselves, the houseparents taught practical skills like bed-making and insisted on good table manners. Although the meals were always good, Carson remembers sitting alone at the supper table after everyone else had left, looking at a plateful of liver—"this detested food"—which he had refused to eat. "I don't remember who won," he says. However, given the structure of the place, I imagine that he soon learned to eat what was put on his plate.

During the two years the twins lived in this dorm, they

Tina and the twins. Note hearing aid on harness.

made steady gains in language until the spring of 1964, when they made a sudden leap forward. When they came home one weekend in April, they were unusually quiet.

"Don't talk so loud," Craig told me. And when we went out for a walk on the farm, Carson complained, "It's so noisy!" Only after some puzzlement did I finally discover what he meant; a flock of migrating birds was singing in the trees nearby.

For the first time in their lives, Craig and Carson were hearing the sounds of spring, amplified in their deaf ears by large black boxes that now hung from white harnesses on their chests. They were wearing their first hearing aids. All weekend their hands were on the dials, first turning the knobs up until their heads crackled with static noise, then turning them down again until their ears subsided into the familiar quiet in which they felt more secure. Now when I began to scold them for something, they merely tuned me out; there was a new source of power in those black boxes!

Of course, it wasn't easy for them to get used to the restrictions of the harness and earpiece. For months they were apt to suddenly yank off the whole apparatus and leave it where it fell. More than one expensive earmold was lost in the haymow. The conspicuous visibility of the aids caused some embarrassment in public. Craig remembers that people would often stop and ask him if he was listening to the radio; when he tried to explain, they would just smile awkwardly and sidle away.

Their teachers noticed that the aids made an immediate difference in the twins' behavior. They became much quieter now that they had a better idea of how much noise they produced. Their comprehension of sound also improved. The progress report at the end of the year proudly noted that with the aid, "Carson responds to whistling, even when the whistler's back is turned to him." And Craig, the teacher said, "responds accurately to material presented approximately 2 or 3 feet from him."

Although this is hardly the description of a miracle, it does indicate an improvement in the twins' use of their hearing. Further, it raises the question of why they were not equipped with aids sooner in their training. The school had known from tests conducted at least a year earlier that the boys had a more severe hearing loss than was originally estimated.

The reason for delay was prescribed by McGinnis in her Method: until an aphasic child had the rudiments of language, amplification would only increase his confusion by subjecting him to unwanted background noise. For better or worse, then, Craig and Carson waited until they were seven years old before getting their aids. It is useless to dwell on what a difference it might have made if another set of professionals had given them hearing aids while they were still babies.

In its third year, 1963-64, Pathway expanded its enrollment to 60 and built a new school in Jeffersonville, 25 miles from Philadelphia. In the fourth year of their schooling, the twins lived in a dormitory on the new campus.

By this time Craig and Carson had a much greater range of expression. They were saying and writing: "The yellow chair is bigger than the green chair"; "Hot is the opposite of cold"; "Juice is a liquid, nylon is a solid"; "On St. Patrick's Day people have parades, sing songs, dance Irish jigs and wear green shamrocks."

Selected entries from the class "News Book" show growth in the children's descriptive powers:

> The little boys and girls played with slinky toys.
> Yesterday the children played near poison ivy.
> Gail has a picture postcard of a poodle dog.
> Craig stood on his head for a long time.

Santa will come in eight days.
Tomorrow the big children will take a test.
Andrea is selling Girl Scout cookies.
Phyllis has pink socks.
Yesterday Pat washed my face with snow.
Gail sneezed many times.
A rocket is going to the moon.

The boys' unsupervised language was admittedly more labored, as shown by a card from Craig when he was eight years old:

Dear mother and daddy,

I am sad because I want to go home. I play a games in the gym today after school. I did not fight maybe and I color this paper of bad picture at the school. I swim one day.

Love,
Craig

At the end of the fourth year, 1964-65, the staff at Pathway decided that Carson (8) was ready to enter the second grade of a school for hearing children. After some deliberation we finally chose for him the private Lancaster Christian Day School, which is located only a few miles from our home. Craig, however, had lagged slightly behind Carson and needed one more year at Pathway.

This brought the rivalry between the boys to a new pitch. "Eventually," says Craig frankly, "I grew to dislike Carson very much."

Carson admits, "I thought I was smarter than Craig. I felt he was holding me back."

When Craig began his final year of special schooling, he was depressed by the feeling that he had failed somehow, although he was never sure just what he had done wrong. Fortunately he had a teacher who was determined to bolster his self-confidence.

"What I tried to give him that year was the feeling that he was special," Lois Sternberg recalls. "After he had done some work, he would say, 'I don't want to do that; it's not right,' or he would even say, 'Carson is smarter. Carson can do it better.' Then I would take him by the shoulders and say, 'You're the smartest person in this school, and I expect great things of you.' "

Carson was an achiever who drove himself hard, demanding the respect of his teachers. In contrast, Craig was more shy, and people gave him affection.

"Oh, he made me laugh sometimes," Lois remembers. "When I would give him a book, he'd sigh and say, 'Another book—everyone gives me books.' I felt like hugging him."

Gradually, Craig did become more self-assured. At the

Tina and Grandma Glick look on as Craig and Carson blow out the candles, first on one birthday cake and then the other.

91

end of the year Lois wrote a glowing report on him, noting, "He has become aware of his abilities and his friends and announces an error with a grin and, 'Oh, I made a mistake!' "

Everyone agreed that Craig had completed his course at Pathway in the spring of 1966. Now he too could finally come home to live with us again.

Our family feels a great deal of gratitude toward Pathway School. We sensed a deep concern there for all of us and appreciated the general openness of the staff. To be sure, the Method—which was gospel for a few years—soon lost its validity and the aphasic division of the school was actually discontinued after Craig's last year. But the individual teacher is more important than any method will ever be, and there were some very good teachers at Pathway.

Looking back, I am increasingly aware of the risks that we, parents and educators, took. We gambled on the chance that Craig and Carson would learn to speak—that is, we did not make available to them the manual language that would have made communication easier. We pushed them hard to become "normal," to be like us, and thereby may have partly denied the fact that they would be forever deaf. We put a lot of pressure on those two little boys.

At the time, it seemed that all our gambles paid off. Pathway had given the boys usable speech and a great determination to succeed. Now they had to prove themselves in the hearing world.

Chapter 9

On Friday of his first week at a hearing school, Craig sat in his seat in the middle of what seemed to him an enormous classroom. For the entire week he had been in a daze from trying to concentrate on the ceaseless activity around him, as though he were the spinning hub of a wheel over which he had no control.

The teacher gave him book after book, and he was staggered by the implication that he would have to read all of them; class followed class in such rapid succession he could barely find the right page before it was time to turn to another. He could snatch only an occasional word from the constant movement of the teacher's lips. When she asked a question, hands went up all over the room, and then some child would give an incomprehensible answer before Craig knew what the question had been. He was numb with fear that the teacher would call on him; when she did, he struggled desperately to read or say something that would satisfy her and turn the excruciating attention of the room away from him.

He did not really understand why he had left Pathway, where he had been so much more comfortable. There Lois had repeated everything slowly when he didn't understand, and he had been, after Carson left, the star of a small group of students. At Pathway he had never really had to do homework, but here he had to go on struggling at night with tutors and assignments.

Craig was not aware that he was the only child in the room who had such difficulty following the discussion. At Pathway all the children had problems with communication, and Craig assumed that at least some of the other children in his new school were like him also. He assumed that some of them, too, gleaned their comprehension of speech from the visual clues of moving lips. His perception of the other students was still blurred. By the end of the first week he still did not know—not having heard—the names of the other children, and he had certainly not categorized them into groups of "hearing" and "deaf" or "normal" and "handicapped." While he knew he and Carson had special problems with their ears, signified by their hearing aids, he had no clear idea of what it meant to be deaf or aphasic.

Surely other children in the class had the same means of comprehension that he had—but they had simply learned better then he how to read those lips, moving endlessly around him. He could only conclude he was slower than the other children, not as smart. After all, Carson too had a hearing aid, but Carson found it easier to talk and understand, and yelled on the playground like everyone else.

It is likely that on the Friday of his first week of school Craig would have daydreamed about the playground and recess, when he could release frustration, run faster than almost anyone else, and sometimes team up with Carson—the two of them were the biggest boys in their class.

At any rate, near the end of the day on Friday, knowing

this was the last day of the week, Craig had finally let down his guard and had lost his focus on the ceaseless movements of the teacher's lips, the arms waving, the mumbled sentences of the other children, the spontaneous unexplainable laughter at an unintelligible joke. Then, suddenly, in his fatigue, he became aware that a new formal proceeding was taking place in the room. As the teacher read off their names, students in turn got up, went to the front of the room, and began to talk. Their lips moved fast, then stumbled, then went on still faster in such a way that Craig knew they were reciting something, but he could not decipher a single word.

It became apparent soon, as child after child went through this odd exercise, that he too would be called upon, and Craig was gripped with terror. What could he do? He had no idea what was expected.

"Craig." The teacher looked at him; he rose obediently, numb with dread, and went to her desk. She sat with folded hands, and in front of her was a book which Craig recognized as a Bible. "It's your turn," she said.

Craig stood a moment hoping for some revelation. Nothing happened. He was dumbstruck at the center of the classroom. He broke into tears and went sobbing back to his seat. Only later did he understand that he was supposed to have memorized a Bible verse.

Craig's first week of school in the third grade stands out in his memory as a time of unrelieved misery, and the scene before the judgment bar of the teacher's desk was, he says, one of the most terrifying experiences of his life. I present the scene above because it shows how desperately frustrating a simple demand for communication can be to a deaf child if he does not understand. I hasten to add, however, that this scene does not give a full picture of the twins' experiences at their elementary school. Many of the teachers there took extra time to help the boys understand their lessons. Before Craig and Carson came into their respective classes, the teachers urged the other children to be helpful, according to the Christian principles of the school, and in general there was no discrimination against the twins there. They were treated in a wholesome manner, helpful but not condescending.

I'm sure, also, that the teacher who put Craig through such misery over the Bible verses was quite unaware of how confusing this situation was for him. She simply assumed he had understood her when she made the assignment. It is even possible that she asked him whether he understood and, in his bewilderment and desire to please, he nodded that he did. It was in fact almost inevitable that, by attending a hearing school staffed by teachers untrained in how to communicate with deaf children, Craig and Carson would go through some excruciating times of incomprehension; one might well ask whether deaf children like Craig and Carson should attend hearing schools, where they are so certain to be frustrated.

Vernon and I were troubled throughout the twins' elementary years with various forms of this central question of whether we had chosen the right schooling for them. "How much do they understand? How much will they ever understand? Are we pushing them too hard?" we wondered.

Vernon and I were used to the tension that sometimes radiated from the boys' faces and bodies as they labored to force their desires and ideas through the narrow channels of their slowly developing speech. We remembered the years when they had almost no speech, and their energy had short-circuited through their hyperactive bodies. At least by the time they entered elementary school, they did have speech, halting though it was.

To a perceptive person meeting the twins for the first time however, their frustration could still be almost frightening. "At first I thought, 'They're time bombs!' I could tell they were very intelligent, but especially with Craig there was the feeling—'if I can't express myself, I'm going to explode!'" Thus Sue Recla, the twins' tutor in fifth and sixth grades, recalls their intensity. She saw them for at least an hour of study after they had already spent a full day of concentration in school.

The explosion Sue feared when she first met the boys never came, perhaps because she was so adept at communicating with them across her kitchen table. In general she was always struck by how eager they were to learn. "It was a pleasure to teach them," she recalls.

Larry, Sue's husband, interjects a note of qualification: "I also remember your tremendous frustration at them."

"But it wasn't frustration directed at them," Sue says. "It was frustration *with* them."

"They were perhaps frustrated," Larry adds. "But they didn't miss a thing. Those eyes! Those eyes!"

Another tutor and babysitter we had over the years, Barbara Huddle Ressler, kept a diary, in which she occasionally noted some trying evenings with the boys. One entry shows Craig as he continued to wrestle with his Bible-verse assignments; on this particular evening he was trying to twist his tongue into an acceptable rendition of three verses which contained the words "satisfieth" and "executeth."

"He reached a point," says Barbara's diary, "where he would just flop down and give up." Given his fear of humiliation in front of the class, however, it is almost certain that he "executed" and "satisfied" his assignment somehow the next day—even if he didn't know what the words meant.

Vernon and I questioned the value of putting the boys through such bewildering exercises, and we consulted

McGinnis, their former teacher. "Oh, it'll be good for them," she said. "Anything to exercise their speech." Guided, or perhaps misguided, by the general principle that repetitive exercises were beneficial, we even had the boys take piano lessons for a while. Barbara recalls how angry they would get when they made mistakes on the key board—even though, with so little hearing, the only way they knew they had made an error was to see their fingers hit the wrong keys.

At home we continued to work on their speech, which had been steadily improving but was still awkward. Scenes such as the following were common:

The time is after school. The boys have been with a tutor for an extra hour and after quick glasses of milk are going outside to play.

"I . . . go . . . ball," says Craig.

"I am going to play ball," I correct him.

"I go playing ball," he says, sidling out the door.

"No, look," I say, emphasizing each word, "I am going. . . ."

"I . . . am . . . go-ing. . . . I . . . am going play ball," he says halfway across the porch.

"Supper is almost ready," I say. But his back is turned, and in just a few steps he is completely out of reach of my voice. The only way I could get his attention now would be to run after him screaming, and this hardly seems appropriate. I will have to go out and find him later.

We are in a restaurant. The waitress is impatient. "What do you want?"

"A ha-am-bur-ghur."

"A what?" she asks over the smash of dishes in the kitchen. nearby.

"Louder," we say to the embarrassed boy.

"A ham-bur-ghur."

"And salad," I add.

"What kind of dressing?" She looks at me, but I resist the temptation and look at the tense boy.

"What . . . kind . . . of . . . dressing?" I say slowly.

He says something that sounds like "French."

"French," I say with resignation. When the salad comes, of course it is not what he wanted at all.

We have planned a trip to the Hershey Amusement Park on Saturday and as usual have evoked the rule that all school assignments must be done before we go. The twins are working on their math but don't understand something in their books and ask us to help. Tina is wailing that it's not fair for her to wait because *they* haven't done their work. Vernon and I have been trying to close the store, but a customer dawdles from one stereo set to another. Finally he leaves. Then we sit down and painstakingly spell our way through the math lesson before we pack up and go to the park.

Lancaster Christian Day School was run according to principles of order based on old-fashioned theology. It was the kind of place where children lined up in rows to recite or get a drink of water and where learning and memorization were often regarded as being synonymous. In many respects this emphasis on structure made it easier for the boys to adapt to hearing school. They were used to the regimentation of the McGinnis Method, and repetitive learning was easier, given the limits of their language comprehension. "For a long time all I understood was action, to follow the other kids and fall into patterns," recalls Carson. At Lancaster Christian these patterns were clearly defined.

In general the teachers at the school made a conscious effort to treat Craig and Carson as "normal" children; the rationale was in part based on the diagnosis that the boys were aphasic, and aphasia was presumed to be more curable than something like deafness. One former teacher says she forced herself to treat Carson as much like the other children as possible. Even though reading aloud was painful for him, she deliberately called on him at least as often as the other children, and she rapped his knuckles if he misbehaved.

There was of course the danger that too much rigid structure and memorization would limit the twins' mental development. "Their learning was bascially parroting at that time," recalls tutor Sue Recla.

Vernon and I were particularly concerned that the twins might never learn the complex and abstract ideas about religion that meant so much to us. We were glad that the school tried to operate according to religious principles. We were, however, somewhat apprehensive that the boys might, in their uncritical zeal to learn, take in too literally the particular brand of religion which permeated the school. We did not agree with some details of the school's theology.

During the time when blacks were marching for their rights in Mississippi, our church held a black-studies course, and Vernon and I relayed some of our concerns about racial injustice to the boys. When Martin Luther King was assassinated, we discussed the event with them and expressed our horror. Craig brought up the subject at school. The teacher shook her finger at him. "Martin Luther King was a *troublemaker*," she said.

Craig came home in distress, barely able to articulate his frustration. We told him quite plainly that his teacher was wrong. "People have different ideas about things," we told him. "And even your teachers are wrong sometimes. You must learn to think for yourself."

Every child has to learn to think for himself, of course, but it is especially difficult for deaf children to get varied intellectual perspectives that make independent thought possible. The boys were for a long time more naive than children who had greater language facility. The King incident was a real turning point for Craig; he was disillusioned and puzzled but certainly stronger and less gullible in the end.

Carson also was moved deeply by the King assassination. We all went to see a movie about the black leader, made after his death. "I could sympathize with the blacks because

I had not been treated equally, because of my handicap. I was labeled as handicapped but didn't really feel I was helpless. I had dreams of betterment for myself as well as for the blacks," Carson recalls. The movie brought him to tears. "I could understand the words of Martin Luther King very well. He was easy to lip-read. It was very powerful and the music built up too so I could feel it. When he died, and in the funeral march, I cried."

Carson must have been about 12 years old when he saw this film. I suspect that his recollection of the film is described in terms he has picked up since then, and that at the age of 12 he could not have articulated so clearly that he was handicapped and thus identified with disadvantaged blacks. Nevertheless, it is obvious that his personal awareness of being handicapped had reached a conscious level by this time.

It is very difficult for any of us in the family to recall very precisely when and how we came to define their handicap as

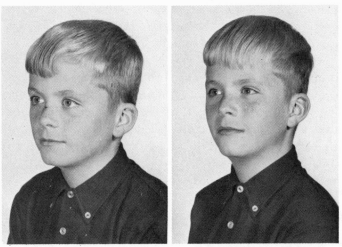

Craig (left) and Carson at Lancaster Christian Day School.

deafness. When the boys began hearing school, we were still telling teachers and other interested persons that the problem was aphasia. However, I have an indelible memory of Craig, at an early age, standing in his room and screaming, "I don't want to be deaf!"

Gradually throughout the elementary years, as Pathway and McGinnis fell further into the past, we dropped the term "aphasia" and began using the more direct term of "deafness," or the somewhat evasive term "hearing loss," which, while accurate, can easily become a euphemism. We—including the boys—used both terms for many years, reflecting our own ambiguous feelings about the kind of handicap we were dealing with and the chances of "overcoming" it. But yearly visits to Dr. Rosenberg, our audiologist, brought us finally to an accurate picture of the twins' hearing problem, to a diagnosis of deafness, as time and again the doctor drew the same audiograms at the bottom of the chart.

Unfortunately, throughout their elementary and highschool years, the twins had very little contact with other deaf people. The few early contacts they did have were, by coincidence, dramatic and even frightening.

When Craig was very young, a cousin of mine who was deaf came to visit. He is a man who gestures a great deal and communicates usually with the hearing world by exchanging written notes. Vernon had learned how to finger-spell from a deaf employee on his uncle's farm, so he and the visitor communicated partly in this fashion. The deaf man, as usual, was very animated.

"I didn't know who this man was, who was flailing his hands about," Craig recalls. "I hid under some furniture."

Then, heightening the drama of the scene, a thunderstorm struck and the electricity was cut off. We lit candles and continued to write and pass notes, peering at them by the dim candlelight. Craig observed this scene from his hiding place in a shadowy corner of the room. "I was terrified!" he says.

Carson remembers a similar scene, when one night Grandpa Glick took him and Craig to a church for the deaf near our home. The boys were about ten years old. Here again the scene was surrounded by darkness, and the movement of hands, as the congregation sang together in sign language, created a strange confusion of light and shadow. "It was night," recalls Carson. "I was short; everyone was tall and seemed to tower up and overshadow me, with their hands moving above me."

Already by this time, without the knowledge of Vernon or me, Carson had developed the idea, apparently at Pathway School, that sign language was inferior to speech. "I did pick up somewhere back at that time—never, never learn sign language; it's not good for you; it will make you dumb. Deaf people use sign language and they're dumb. For a long time I was careful not to play dumb, or be dumb, whatever that meant. I tried to learn speech. And I didn't think I was deaf, because deaf people were dumb and I wasn't dumb."

This was not a reflection of any clear prejudice that Vernon and I had against sign language, but we did not make any effort during the boys' elementary years to have them learn what, according to many current researchers, is the "native language" of deaf children.

One reason we didn't feel a need for sign language was simply that, even as the boys grew up, we continued to be unaware of what it offered. Education for the deaf was still overwhelmingly oral. Second, it seemed that the boys' development of speech and lipreading skills was so successful that sign language would have been extraneous.

As the time approached for the twins to leave Pathway, we did consider the possibility of sending them to a school

103

for the deaf, or another special school, and we asked Dr. Rosenberg what he thought.

"Give it a try at hearing school," he said, although he didn't sound particularly optimistic. Only as the years went by did he become more excited. "Don't change what you're doing. They shouldn't be doing this well. Keep it up!"

In light of his assessment many years ago, Dr. Rosenberg's current summation of the boys' story is ironic: "Your case is one where everything went wrong—and everything turned out right! The twins were diagnosed very late; then they were misdiagnosed and given the wrong kind of training; they didn't get amplification nearly soon enough. Yet, strangely, it all turned out unusually well in the end."

The boys did successfully adapt to hearing school. They did the same work expected of their peers and got good grades. They had friends and enjoyed good social status. Their oral skills improved to a point where they could hold a conversation (if somewhat laborious) with almost anyone on any topic suited to their age.

The elementary years were a period of slow but regular growth, during which Vernon and I began to relax a little. The boys, too, became comfortable at school. Within one year Carson was largely in control of the situation. It took Craig several years longer, and it was always more difficult for him, but by the middle of his elementary years he too was reasonably self-assured. This progress was largely uneventful, and we never celebrated a final victory over the boys' handicap, but we did become used to hearing glowing compliments on the twins' "success."

I will reflect later on the idea of "success" in oral language, and will have a few final words on the subject of sign language. Suffice it to say here that the "success" of elementary school did have its limits, as is evident in Craig's rather pathetic recollection of the distance he sometimes felt between him and his classmates. "There was a girl in the row right next to mine who seemed attractive to me, but I didn't know who she was, didn't even know her name for several years."

Both boys, especially Craig, were fortunate in being athletic, for this was an important way in which they gained prestige within their peer group. When the twins reached junior-high age, however, the social life of their classmates began to change. Push-and-shove games between the boys and girls gave way to the first moves of formal dating. Playground games turned into more serious sports, and now there were more groups of kids doing nothing but talking, talking, talking—in the classroom, on the bus, on the phone. Craig and Carson were not completely left out. Craig remembers how the ninth-grade girls on the bus used to giggle and ask him and Carson to sit with them. The girls were apparently attracted to these two self-possessed boys, who had an air of being different. The boys were flattered and went along with the games. "But I didn't really understand the idea of 'going with a girl' or 'sitting with a girl,'" Craig recalls. "I had no concept about dating."

Thus, while I was, and continue to be, grateful for the degree to which both boys learned speech, I have also learned that the fact of deafness never goes away. The high-school years would show the obvious fact that good grades do not restore hearing.

As I recall the atmosphere of our home during the elementary and much of the high-school years, I immediately detect two sources of tension which were so much a part of life then that we took them for granted. It has taken years of change for all of us to get perspective on these issues, and only recently have we really articulated them. They were themes that are certainly common in many family dramas:

first, rivalry between the parents' "need" to work and the children's desire for attention; second, sibling rivalry in its various forms. Quite frankly I am not entirely sure how to relate these problems in our own family to the presence of deafness. Clearly, deafness was not the sole cause for our conflicts. I think, however, that deafness did heighten them.

Even yet, if the children want to hurt us, they need only say, "You didn't spend enough time at home." And it is painful for me to admit that in fact there were few evenings that we all spent together as a family. Almost every evening Vernon and I worked in the growing audio shop that stood about a hundred feet away from the house. We were both convinced at the time that only through such long hours of work could we ensure the family of a reasonable income. My presence in the shop was necessary because the business had no money to hire extra help. I can see now, however, that I used the work partly as an excuse to escape the limitations of home. To state this confession more positively—I needed something to do in which I could measure my success more easily.

At home I didn't always feel I was succeeding. We should have—but didn't—sat down and looked at the boys' whole history and said, "Look, there's a lot of progress here." Instead, it often seemed we were caught in an interminable struggle from which it was impossible to relax; so we were attracted to the relatively simple business world, where at the end of a day or a year we could calculate our progress on the ledger.

Thus, the twins and Tina spent many evenings at home with the baby-sitter, and over the years they grew to resent their plight. Strangely, I don't think we were conscious of the irony that often, while we sold exquisitely tuned sound and communications systems on one side of the driveway, some child was yelling for attention at an upstairs window across the way, closed in his own world of silence.

I am all too aware of these past absurdities now; I do not, however, think there was an easy solution to the problems. Vernon and I did need to work, and some conflicts were inevitable. Nor am I sure that our exhausted presence at home would have been necessarily beneficial. Our energies were not limitless, nor were we saints. We were tired mentally and emotionally from the unrelenting struggle to help the twins communicate with the world. Call it selfish if you will, but we felt a normal need to get out of the house, breathe a different air, and communicate with the world ourselves.

Although Vernon and I managed to escape the tensions of the household for these evening periods, there seemed to be no such respite for the children, and the house often resounded with sibling discord. "Normal" rivalry was compounded by the pressures of deafness and twinship. Driving themselves hard to succeed and be accepted in the hearing world, the boys turned inevitably to each other for comparison, and the competition between them was persistent for years.

Rivalry between twins is legendary, and it is interesting that Carson, who was in grade school the more literate twin, turned to biblical stories about twins to explain his own feelings. The most elemental story, of course, is that of Cain and Abel, but the implications of this tragedy were too dreadful for Carson: "In the story of Cain and Abel, Cain murdered his brother, and I didn't want to be guilty of that. So I identified instead with the story of Jacob and Esau."

This Old Testament story involves competition between twins for the family "birthright," which was in ancient times a wonderful package of blessings, family power, and a majority of the father's wealth, conferred always upon the eldest son. Esau, having come out of the womb first, was the elder twin and thus was entitled to the birthright, but Jacob, the wily "supplanter," tricked his simpleminded brother into selling the birthright for a bowl of soup one day when Esau came in hungry from hunting. Jacob further tricked his blind father into administering the formal blessing upon himself instead of upon Esau.

Both Craig and Carson knew that Craig had been born first, and this fact had an exaggerated importance for them. "But Jacob got the birthright because he manipulated his family," Carson remembers thinking. "Esau was so dumb to sell the birthright. I always identified with Jacob. I wanted to be the strong one, the smarter one, the dominant one." Carson was not quite sure what the birthright was in our family but felt somehow it meant the "right to be first, to have everything better."

I was quite unaware at the time that Carson was brooding over this story. He remembers asking me once whether there was a birthright in our family. "Oh, no," I laughed, "we don't do that anymore."

Perhaps I should not have dismissed the question so lightly. Was it possible that in a sense we did favor Craig, the older brother? It was true that the personalities of Craig and Carson fit, to an extent, the roles of Jacob and Esau. Craig was more physical, more athletic, while Carson was more intellectual. Craig had more trouble communicating, was not so quick in his studies, and was more obviously frustrated, while Carson was more articulate and seemed more confident. In response to these differences we did sometimes give Craig more reassurance because he seemed to need it more.

There was more than one reason why Carson was so fascinated with the story of Jacob and Esau, and perhaps our family should reread this biblical passage, because it seems to have many similarities to our own history. Certainly in a way Carson's obsession with the birthright was related to his deep feeling that he had somehow been cheated out of the "birthright" of hearing, of normality. The only way he could hope to secure this blessing was by being more alert, more clever than anyone else. Further, an important element of the story is that the father is blind; and while I am not eager to make a comparison between the feeble father in the Bible story, and Vernon and me as parents, it is unfortunately true that we did have our blind spots.

Apparently, back when Carson identified so strongly with the story, it ended for him with Jacob's clever theft of the birthright and the ensuing bitter enmity between the brothers. But I think it is time now for us to complete the story. After many years Jacob and Esau reconciled.

All this analysis of the past is important, even necessary, it seems, because all our children in their later years have felt compelled to articulate their early psychological struggles,

Craig and Carson having fun. Look closely.

and it has taken a lot of talking to relieve old tensions we ignored too long. However, it would be highly inaccurate for me to describe our early family life as a gloomy psychodrama. We all led active lives, and there was lots of light, air, and laughter in our farmhouse on Hobson Road.

On hot summer days the boys and Tina would watch the clock to see when their hour after lunch was up, and then, when the minute hand released them, they would run screaming out the door into the backyard and plunge into a small swimming pool we had put up for them. The neighbor children came too, and they all played "shark" until they were waterlogged. Then they raced for the nearby empty barn to play hide-and-seek or I spy. They crawled through secret passages (the old grain chutes) and constructed mazes with boxes from the audio shop, or swung on iron rings, dropping finally into a bed of hay.

We lived in the old Glick-family farmhouse, shaded by a huge maple tree full of starling nests. There was a large macadamed area—the old barnyard—that covered the area between the house, barn, and audio shop. The boys and Tina raced their bikes here, and sometimes we laughed at them so hard we couldn't bear to watch them anymore. Since they were not quite in command of their brakes, it was their accepted pattern to zoom around the maple tree and run into the side of the house to stop.

On rainy days or in the winter they often played in the large sun-room just off the dining room. Somehow a neighbor had talked us into accepting a pet monkey he could no longer cope with, and Robert, with his sloping forehead, light hair, and dark skullcap, was often to be found swinging from the curtain rods in the sun-room. He would unhook the drapes and then race around the house when we scolded him. He regularly bit the picture frames on the wall and once plastered himself with applesauce on the table.

110

Most often he picked fights with Pepper, our Chihuahua, and quarreled with her for custody of her puppies. We all took this commotion as matter of course. Perhaps we had been so shell-shocked by the boys' early activity that even Robert's hijinks seemed like a normal part of family life.

We had visitors several times a week, because there were so many members of our large extended families living near us, and I thought nothing of setting a dozen places at the table. We in turn often ate meals at Vernon's parents' home just across the fields. The boys got a great deal of attention and were included in conversation at these events.

We often went camping as a family on weekends. Once we made a trip to Baie Verte, Newfoundland, to visit old friends and let the boys see where they had been born. Carson still remembers "the little clinic and, up the hill, the plain town. I really got to like it, my hometown; it had sentimental value for me." Craig, who now dreams of living a more "primitive" life in the country, thought that the people in Newfoundland seemed more content with their lives. In any event, our visit was a big occasion in the village. "We were treated almost like heroes," Carson recalls. I held my breath as the boys played with the local children down on the rocks by the wharf. And when we visited Wild Cove, accessible only by sea, I once looked out into the bay to see the boys and a new friend of theirs far out in a boat, almost in the open ocean. This was yet another occasion on which I held my breath and watched them explore at a distance beyond my control.

There is one scene from that period of our lives, however, that I would choose as being even more representative of the past, with all its frustrations and the mistakes we made in spite of good intentions; but perhaps what is more important is that this scene shows the energy and comic relief we enjoyed.

One day we were expecting visitors from Philadelphia, a couple whom we had never met, who had a child with some "problem." They had heard about us and asked whether they might come and get our advice. Tired of waiting, the boys and Tina decided they wanted a pony-cart ride, and Vernon obligingly hitched up our pony. Lightning was a very spirited animal, who had to be harnessed behind closed doors in the forebay of the barn; only when the buckles were secure could the doors be opened, and even then the pony would bolt out so wildly that the driver could expect a ten-minute fight before things settled into place.

On this particular day someone made a mistake in hitching one side of the cart. When the pony lunged out of the barn, Vernon—alone in the driver's seat—discovered he had no control. A pull on the reins simply banged the cart against the pony's backside, sending him into an even worse panic. Vernon, pony, and cart went bouncing wildly out over a plowed field, and the boys ran yelling after him into the distance.

At this point the couple from Philadelphia arrived. I have no idea what I said as the pony ran into a fence on the far side of the field, bringing the whole circus to an abrupt halt. After our bedraggled family had bumped its way back over the field, and the kids started their bicycle races outside, and the monkey swung from the curtain rods inside, and Pepper yipped ferociously to defend her puppies, I doubt that Vernon or I delivered a reasoned analysis to the troubled parents of the effect of deafness on family relationships, or of the various avenues of education for the handicapped.

But if we were a little weak on analysis in those days, we did develop one means of coping that was no doubt even more important. If the visiting parents that day didn't learn any infallible formula for dealing with their child's handicap, I hope they did have a good laugh.

Chapter 10

Whom we moved out of the old farmhouse in 1969, we transported our furniture on a tractor-drawn wagon to a newer, suburban house, which was in the woods but within sight of busy U.S. Route 30 on the east side of Lancaster. Our mixed rural and suburban life was indicative of a process that was taking place in Lancaster County generally, a process of suburbanization that was changing certain branches of the traditionally conservative Mennonite Church. Vernon and I had joined one of the less traditional congregations. We moved, however, close to the conservative Lancaster Mennonite High School, which the boys began to attend when they reached the ninth grade.

"LMH" was further up along the Millstream, a short walk from our house through a bird sanctuary that resounded in the spring with cries of pheasants or, if you happened to be deaf, was merely filled with the flurry of wings in the tall trees. The campus was pleasant, dominated by large shade trees along the creek. The buildings, like most Mennonite churches and institutions, were constructed of what Carson

113

calls "Mennonite brick," plain and red, with very white mortar.

Both Craig and Carson were eager to attend. LMH was closer to our home, was a large high school, and it offered a driver's training course, which attracted the twins. Since they were used to the strict rules of their parochial elementary school, the highly regulated life at LMH did not at first disturb them. The Christian atmosphere of the school continued to shelter the boys in many ways. Here, as at Lancaster Christian, they found many teachers and students who were basically sympathetic to them. Both twins, especially Craig, had several important religious experiences while attending the school. Carson and Craig continued to get good grades. Both were successful in sports, especially Craig, who eventually was on the varsity soccer team. Carson was class treasurer as a freshman, and class representative in his freshman and junior years.

After all our fretting and worry about homework through all of elementary school, I was tempted to sit back now and assume the twins were safely on the academic rails. When LMH teachers announced a day on which parents could visit classes, I must admit I felt there really wasn't much reason to attend. I did dutifully go, however—and suddenly I was scared all over again. The material was complicated, and I knew the boys couldn't follow the frequent class discussions. I came home and told Vernon, "I bet they're not getting 90 percent of what's being said in class."

This figure of 90 percent loss is exactly what Carson and Craig themselves use in describing their degree of classroom comprehension. It was something they lived with throughout their schooling. And despite their alert readiness to talk to other students, they began to lose some social contact as their classmates entered the teenage telephone-dating stage.

So much had to be explained to the twins in order for them to keep up with the currents of conversation that now swept around them. A simple joke often had to be reconstructed before they too could laugh. And how many jokes can hold their humor after laborious explanation?

Carson remembers an occasion when several friends were having dinner with us. One friend, who has a reputation for being blunt, made one of her typical direct remarks.

"You're subtle," someone else said, and we all laughed.

"What, what was that?" the twins asked.

We repeated the remark. The boys' faces showed complete lack of comprehension.

"Do you know the word 'subtle'?" I asked. "S-u-b-t-l-e." I spelled it a second time.

"Sub-tul," Carson said finally. "Oh, yes, I've read that word. What does it mean?"

"Tactful." Still no light of recognition. "It means someone has tact ..., it means ... to be polite ...; no, it means ... not to be obvious ... ah...."

Finally Carson seemed to understand. "Who is sub-tul?" he asked.

"Sut-le."

"Who is sut-le??"

"We said Kathy is subtle," I said, trying to smile again. "But we really meant the opposite, that Kathy *isn't* subtle, because Kathy said...."

Carson finally gave a polite little laugh. "I've seen that word, but I never knew what it meant," he said. Nobody made any more jokes for a while.

It is a temptation, or shall we say it is simply logical, for deaf people in a hearing world to ask their hearing relatives and friends to interpret for them what is being said. Carson remembers one friend in elementary school whom both he and Craig besieged with questions: "We asked, 'What was that?'—'What's happening?'—too often, and she dropped us. I realized I was losing her friendship. So I stopped, even though it was very hard for me to talk about something else rather than ask questions. Our parents and teachers had always said, 'Ask people; how will you know unless you ask?' So I asked and asked, but I guess I was overbearing sometimes. Here I had to force myself *not* to ask. It took about a year to win that girl's friendship back. She never said anything, but it was clear to me why she was avoiding us, because she was very friendly at first and then started snapping back."

At LMH, Craig first became conscious of how much he was missing in group conversations. He remembers his father's advice at that time: "One time after I had been so frustrated at being left out, Dad told me, 'What they are talking about is not that important. It might be gossiping or bickering, but it's not that important.' So for a while, when people would ask me why I wasn't saying anything, I would comment, 'Well, what you're talking about is not all that important.' They would all crack up and laugh and agree with me."

This consolation was short-lived. Craig realizes, "I did miss out, and still do, because what you talk about with other people is really an interaction, a part of socializing, and if you don't do it well, you miss out. This happened over and over and over all the way through my life."

By the time Craig and Carson were at LMH, they were sensitive to the problem of depending too much on their friends. Nancy Landis and Sharon Buckwalter, friends of both boys in that era, remember their determined independence. The twins continued to make friends more easily among the girls, perhaps partly because girls of that age tend to be more openly sympathetic to people's "problems." Some of the girls were also attracted to Craig's and Carson's air of being different. "Most boys at school were interested only in sports and cars," Nancy says, "but Craig and Carson had other interests—hiking, biking, signing. . . . They knew people from other areas."

"Their attitude was great," recalls Sharon. "They were disciplined and seemed more mature than most students. I don't remember ever seeing them really depressed. They were positive. They were tall and it was good to see their faces coming toward you across the campus."

Nancy remembers how interested they were in talking, how intently they watched every word. Once in the dining hall she was enunciating so clearly, as Carson watched her closely, that a band snapped off her dental braces and hit his mashed potatoes.

Most of the boys' contacts were at school. We tried to have someone at home as much as possible to answer the phone for them, and we made calls by proxy when they asked. There were never many calls, however. Even gregarious Nancy recalls, "I hesitated to call the house, because everything would have to go through you or Tina, so it was easier to see them at school."

Craig and Carson did begin to learn sign language in their early high-school years, thanks largely to Elvin Stoltzfus, who was the pastor of the local (signing) Mennonite Church for the Deaf and also a teacher at the Delaware School for the Deaf. We had always been concerned that Craig and Carson learn about Christianity and had turned to Elvin as the logical person to talk to the boys on the subject: He knew from his own experience with deaf people how important it was for Craig and Carson to sign; while he did not lecture us on the subject, he soon had the boys attending a small, signing club. The boys and their friend Nancy also took sign-language classes at the Hearing Conservation Center in Lancaster. Carson was especially eager to learn, and he and

117

Nancy practiced their new private language often at school.

Signing was a kind of hobby for Carson and was not, at this point, a spectacular breakthrough in communication. Sign, a complicated language, is learned as any other language—slowly. Both Craig and Carson were still basically anchored in the world of speech. In Carson's second year at LMH, Nancy—who was then teaching a sign-language course of her own—asked him to describe to her class what it meant to be deaf.

"I'm not deaf," he said. Then he thought a moment. "I guess I am," he admitted, and later patiently explained to the class what he could and couldn't hear, and what it was like not to be able to use the telephone.

We were all describing the twins now, with very little equivocation, as deaf. This did not necessarily mean, however, that Craig and Carson fully accepted their condition. Craig in particular was struggling to assert himself.

From the time he was in eighth grade until he was in eleventh grade, Craig worked summers at Camp Hebron, a church-run recreational area for young people. Of these summers he says, "I was on my own. The last year I was head lifeguard. I started as the youngest worker, and many others on the staff were college age. I could do a lot of things the campers my own age couldn't do." Craig gained confidence at Camp Hebron. He also had several experiences while there that affected his view of his deafness.

Craig sat in an open field near the Conestoga Christian Day School in Morgantown, Pennsylvania, with other young people, eager to hear a talk by Nicky Cruz, a reformed "gangster" from New York City. Craig had traveled to the three-day outdoor Christian youth meeting with other staff members and campers from Camp Hebron. He had read Nicky Cruz's book *Run Baby Run* and was keyed to a high degree of suspense in anticipation of the speech.

As usual when he sat in large groups of people, Craig paid little attention to the crackle and rumble of the people walking and talking around him. Suddenly, however, he had a sense of moving further off into his own separate world. People were still milling nearby, their mouths were still moving, but everything seemed to be growing quieter, as though the volume of noise were being steadily turned down.

Panic-stricken, Craig realized that the batteries in his hearing aid were going dead. He stumbled through the crowd and raced back toward the dormitory where he and his friends slept, hoping he had brought an auxiliary pack of batteries with him to the school. He panted into his room and fumbled through his pack, throwing his clothes on the floor, then tore through them again in a search which proved to be futile. In his haste to leave he had left the batteries back at Camp Hebron.

He was alone in the dorm. He imagined that the meeting had already begun, could see the speaker walk onstage before the intent audience. The frustration he had felt for years at being alone exploded to an almost unbearable point. "I want to be healed. I don't want to be deaf. I don't want to be deaf!" ran over and over through his mind.

This longing to be healed had been mounting in him, especially during the last few days, because several "miracles" had been performed during the youth conference, and a spirit of faith had been running high among the group.

Craig seized his dying hearing aid and yanked it out of his ear. Then he shut his eyes. "Dear God, please heal me now," he prayed. "I want to hear. I could serve you better; please heal me now." He waited a moment. "But, dear God, if you don't want to heal me now, will you please return the power

119

to the batteries until I hear Nicky Cruz; then I don't care what happens." He opened one eye hesitantly to see whether anything had happened; he looked down at the hearing aid in his hand. An almost overwhelming desire came over him to smash it against the wall. He clenched his fist, but his hand hesitated in midair. "If I still can't hear," he thought sheepishly, "how will I ever explain the broken aid?" He knew how expensive it was.

He put the aid into his ear, ran back to the crowd, and struggled through it to his friends again. Nicky Cruz had just begun talking. Craig was further back in the audience than he had at first thought, and it was difficult for him to follow the speech; but it did seem to him that the battery power was stronger, and it did hold out for the duration of the service. Then the batteries faded rapidly; and later, on the ride back to camp, when Craig fell into a deep sleep of exhaustion, the hearing aid was dead in his ear.

A year or so later Craig attended a Christian Youth Rally in New York City, where again Nicky Cruz was to be the speaker. After his earlier experience with the ex-gangster in Morgantown, Craig was now desperate to hear him clearly. Unfortunately, he could not get a seat in the front of the room, and he could barely see the mouth of the speaker; still, by sitting on the edge of his chair and peering through a slot between the people in front of him, he could manage to pick up some of the words. Then just after the meeting began a tall black man with an enormous Afro sat down in front of Craig. The bush of hair completely blocked his view.

"Damn him, damn him, damn him!" Craig shouted in-side himself. His eyes filled with tears of frustration, and he sat through the entire service without seeing anything of Nicky Cruz except the top of his head. He lost the speech entirely. "Why did God do this to me?" went through his mind as he sat in hopeless silence; but his guilt at having cursed the black man and at having blamed God for his deafness had grown almost intolerable by the end of the evening.

Afterward, while the rest of his friends were animatedly discussing the service, Craig sank into hopeless dejection. A counselor asked him how he enjoyed the speech. On the spur of the moment Craig burst out, "Why am I deaf?" Then he began to cry.

"God never makes a mistake," the counselor said. Somehow this was the reassurance that Craig needed. Peace came over him as they prayed.

Both Craig and Carson attended Deaf Week at Camp Hebron, which attracted some 50 to 75 young people who either were deaf or hard of hearing. The common language of Deaf Week was sign. Carson enjoyed the chance to practice his signing. Craig was less at ease in this group of deaf people. The third year he attended Deaf Week, the fringes of a large hurricane swept through Pennsylvania bringing several days of heavy rain. The campers were trapped in small buildings in proximity to each other, and cabin fever soon became epidemic. The somewhat theatrical element inherent in signing became more pronounced as physical frustration mounted, or at least this is the way it seemed to Craig. Shy, not quite at home among his deaf peers, Craig began to feel increasingly isolated. He was not nearly as proficient in sign as most of the other campers. Many of them were perhaps less well-educated than he. Unfortunately, all these differences affected his view of sign language itself, as he says now: "It seemed to me they talked about the same things over and over; they talked about 'general' things. That's all they had vocabularies for. They couldn't talk about anything serious. Whenever I talked about anything with feelings, they got exasperated. They exaggerated everything."

At camp Craig became interested in a deaf girl whose most familiar conversational language was sign. He dated her for several years. "I went to a couple of deaf clubs with her but never felt a part of it," he recalls. "And with her it seemed I couldn't communicate my ideas and feelings. Either she couldn't understand my speech; or she'd say, 'Yes, I understand,' but she wouldn't really know what I meant." Craig didn't seem to consider the possibility that this problem in communication with other deaf people, from their point of view, was his own inexperience with sign.

Seen from their more public angle, the twins were tolerant young men, who didn't engage in frequent social bickering among their adolescent peer group. "They never cut other people down," recalls a high-school friend. "They were above that, it seemed." There was certainly a sense in which the twins seemed more mature than many others in their high-school class. They were disciplined students and athletes.

Once they were convinced that they should or should not do something, there was no question about their course of action, no hesitation or self-indulgent compromise. They would lift weights and exercise until they were red in the face. Their conservative religious morality was clear-cut. Their habits were impeccable if not fastidious—no guilty potato chips or chocolate ice cream for them.

This discipline was their proven method of making their way against odds in a hearing world, and it was something a mother could well appreciate. At the same time, I was aware there was another side to this discipline—a certain danger of rigidity and even intolerance. Because, although Craig and Carson seldom gossiped at school, within their own minds they were often ready to condemn anything that violated their own sense of rightness.

Tina remembers driving with Carson once when an approaching car moved over toward their lane. "Watch out!" Tina cried.

"But he's on my side!" said Carson indignantly, refusing to slow down to avert a possible collision. "It's his fault."

The cars missed each other. As usual, Carson had enough good sense to warn him of real danger. Or perhaps he was still protected by that presence Vernon had long ago recognized when he remarked, "Their guardian angels must have ulcers! At any rate I did sometimes worry about the stubborn streak that ran through our family.

"They didn't gossip about other people," the high-school friend says; and then she adds, "If they picked on anyone, it would be each other." This qualification was unfortunately true.

The rivalry between the twins did become less physical and open in their early high-school years. They no longer threatened to throw glass jars or suitcases at each other—to mention two earlier episodes of brotherly disagreement. The conflict changed as the twins became increasingly capable in language. Carson, who had an advantage in being slightly more articulate at this age, often criticized Craig verbally. Craig argued too and had his own quieter ways of showing resentment. They seemed to see the world in different ways, and the limitations of their handicap continued to intensify their rivalry. Someone who has trouble understanding what is happening around him can easily become suspicious or intolerant of differing opinions.

"We often saw the same thing, but we viewed it differently, and whenever we talked about it later, the whole thing would get blown out of proportion," Craig recalls. Unable to reconcile their differences, the twins gradually began to avoid potential disputes and talked with each other less. Most of the conversations between them had to do with practical questions, such as who would get the use of the car

123

on a given weekend. At school they took different classes when possible. They often had the same friends but talked with them separately. And without being able to articulate what was happening, they often engaged in subtle contests to see who could acquire the most, or more popular, friends.

Vernon and I were aware of this rivalry and tried to deal with it. We made sure that the twins were separated for part of each summer so that they could develop individually. We always encouraged them to express their emotions. We never sat down with both boys and discussed their rivalry openly, however, until some years later. I'm not even sure we could or should have done that earlier. Their perceptions and vocabulary were, after all, much more limited than those of other young people of the same age. Their eyes were habitually turned outward to pick up clues from the often incomprehensible world about them. It was only after they began to learn more about psychology that they were capable of analyzing what went on inside their minds.

After two years at LMH, Carson decided to transfer to Eastern Mennonite High School in Harrisonburg, Virginia. His years there would be dramatic and emotional. Craig and Tina stayed at LMH one more year.

Craig did not have a happy junior year at LMH. "My social life fell apart. I had to go out and do something to interest the kids if I wanted to be part of the group; I had to attract them. There was a lot of peer pressure to have a car and girlfriends. After a while I was watching TV every night, wanted to go out and was bored, but couldn't decide how to break my pattern. Finally one night Tina came down and said, 'Why don't you go out, date, get to know people more?'

"So the next week I asked some girls out, but there was a lot of worry about whether I would be rejected or not. I was extremely self-conscious because I was deaf. I was afraid I'd lose the girls to other guys who were not deaf. And it was always hard to have conversations when we were going from one place to another because in the dark I couldn't see what the girl was saying. Also, I couldn't whisper because I would whisper too loud; and they couldn't whisper to me because I couldn't hear them and couldn't look at them while I was driving. Then there was the telephone. I always had to talk to the girls face-to-face, and if their reaction was negative, it would be more painful for me."

During this year Craig and Tina both talked of following Carson to EMHS. Carson was not at first receptive to the idea. He was enjoying his year alone; some of his friends didn't even know he had a twin. In the spring, however, Carson wrote a letter to Craig inviting him to come to EMHS, especially so that Craig could become part of a "charismatic" religious group which Carson had joined. Craig finally decided to transfer. He wanted to break out of the restrictive patterns which seemed to have trapped him. And, in fact, the senior year in Virginia would be a time of new social awareness for both him and Carson.

Chapter 11

Carson glanced up at the mouths of the other five people seated in a circle around him, who, without reliance on any particular melody, were improvising a hymn to God using the words of an Old Testament psalm. Then he looked down at his Bible and sang along with them, knowing that his own singing, tuneful or not, would be absorbed among the freely varied voices of his fellow worshipers:

> Make a joyful noise unto the Lord, all ye lands. Serve the Lord with gladness: come before his presence with singing. . . .

As a member of this charismatic religious group at EMHS, Carson was able for the first time to take close part in a worship service. He had never dared to sing in church, nor had he ever really been able to follow what was said there. But this group was small and informal enough for him to understand more of what was said.

After the psalm was finished, everyone knelt to pray. Carson kept his eyes open to read the lips of the persons praying. This was the most difficult part of the service for him, because often people spoke into the backs of their chairs, so that their mouths were hidden from him. In this most private part of the service, he had to crane his neck to see, scanning the group when one person was finished praying so that he could detect who would address God next; and sometimes, uncomfortable at being the only person with open eyes, he would bow his head quickly in submission, even if this meant he would lose track of what was happening. He prayed aloud himself in most meetings, watching carefully first to be sure no one else was speaking.

After prayer they all got up from their knees, turned, and sat down. There were no preachers or assigned leaders in the group, but one member, Byron, was recognized informally as the most articulate spiritual force among them. As usual, he spoke for a while, supported by the "hallelujahs" and "amens" of the others. His text today was from Acts, one of the most important books of the Bible for this charismatic group, which was trying to return to the miraculous, intimate experience of God's power as it had been manifested in the early apostolic church.

Because today Carson had requested healing, he knelt. Byron placed his hands on Carson's head and prayed, "God, we claim your promise that your healing power will be here with us today as it was with the disciples that walked with Jesus. We ask that you heal Carson now. Restore his hearing. For your honor and your glory. Amen."

"Amen," said everyone.

Carson, head bowed, could not understand what was said above him, although he knew from other services what the words would be. "God, please heal me now," he prayed, and remained kneeling for a while. Then he opened his eyes and looked up. The radiant, expectant eyes of the group fixed on his face.

"Hallelujah!" he read on their lips.

"Amen," he said. "Amen."

For the next several weeks Carson listened each morning when he awoke, to see whether the sounds around him would suddenly ring new and clear. He expected when he prayed that at any time the miracle might occur, and his ears would suddenly open. It was something he had always thought would happen, and now he was sure it would. He always thought in terms of getting his hearing "back," as though he had originally been normal and then lost his hearing later. He felt really so much like a hearing person.

And when his faith was beginning to flag, a friend stopped him one day and said, "God told me last night that you will be able to hear again." To Carson this was an irrefutable promise.

Vernon and I heard about some of these incidents through relatives of ours who lived in Virginia, and as soon as possible we went down to visit Carson. He told us a somewhat abbreviated version of what had happened.

"We know these are all good, sincere people," we said. "But just because you *want* to be healed, and they want you to be healed, doesn't mean necessarily that you *will* be healed. That's up to God."

"I know," he said a little uncertainly. But I could see his mind beginning to close against us, the unbelieving parents.

"And maybe," I went on, "you should think of the healing in a different way." He looked puzzled.

"You have overcome your handicap in many ways," I said. "You aren't so bitter about it anymore. Maybe that could be the healing." His face relaxed slightly.

"Maybe," he said.

This was only one of several "healing" experiences both twins had. Craig attended a few charismatic meetings with Carson. After one, they had a private "healing" session together. They went to Carson's room, claimed Jesus' promise that "wherever two or three are gathered together, there will I be also," and asked God to heal them both. The lack of immediate response did not disturb either of them by this time.

"I was aware," Craig says, "that God answers in many different ways—yes, no, wait. So if nothing happened then, I just knew I would have to wait a little longer."

Craig never really became a member of the charismatic group, and in his second year at EMHS Carson gradually became less involved. One of the things that first caused him to feel less comfortable in the group was, ironically, their strong interest in "speaking in tongues." This practice stems from an apostolic experience, recorded in the book of Acts, in which the earliest Christians spoke spontaneously in strange languages, "as though with tongues of fire." Modern believers in "tongues" (glossolalia) speak out in their meetings in words or syllables that might to some observers seem to be nonsensical; but to the initiated these sounds are profound expressions of prophecy or praise.

Carson, of course, could neither hear nor lip-read these sounds when they were pronounced by other members of his group. He felt some people were pressuring him to speak in tongues himself. But after all his years of trying to articulate, trying to refine the noises he made into recognizable speech, he could not now suddenly deliver such a spontaneous language of his own.

"Hello," I said into the telephone in our kitchen. "This is Mrs. Glick. How are you?. . . Say, there's someone here who wants to talk to you."

I handed the receiver to Craig, who held it in silence until I had gone into the adjacent bedroom and closed the door. He had instructed me to do this before we had made the phone call. Then through the door, in spite of myself, I could hear his husky voice as he talked to his new girlfriend from school, his first girlfriend really, anywhere. They were separated over Christmas vacation, and Craig had shown all the symptoms of being lovesick for days. Finally he had asked me to call the girl. I would have to listen to the girl's side of the conversation. Then I was supposed to leave the room so that Craig could do his talking in private. Now, even on the far side of the bedroom, I could hear him addressing the girl with various forms of endearment.

"Mom, come here." I returned to the kitchen and took the phone again. Craig waited eagerly by my side.

"Hello," I said.

"Hello," the girl said. She paused awkwardly, "Ah ... tell Craig I would like to see him, ah . . . ."

"She says she would like to see you," I repeated slowly to Craig, who grinned.

"Tell him I'm writing him a letter ... ah . . . . Yesterday my whole family was here for dinner . . . ."

"Yesterday her whole family was there for dinner."

"Um, let's see," the girl seemed at a loss for words. "Oh, we have some snow."

"They have snow."

"Tell him, tell him I'll be glad to see him when school starts. . . . I guess I did say that."

"I'm sure he'll be glad to hear it again," I assured her. He was. I left the room again while Craig talked into what was for him a dead receiver. He finally said goodbye—without hearing her reply—and hung up.

I was glad that Craig had found a girl who was responsive to him and patient with his deafness. I liked the girl. But I could see that Craig was headed for disaster.

"Do you have to get so serious so fast?" I asked him. "Why at this rate you'll soon be married," I tried to make

130

this sound like an obvious absurdity.

"You and Dad got married when *you* were 19," he said.

"But maybe *we* were too young." I gave him a little lecture on the dangers of young marriages. It was more difficult, however, for me to express the second, deeper reservation I had about the present relationship. "Do you think you would have trouble communicating with her in any way?" I asked obliquely.

"Oh, no," he said with conviction. "Why should I? She understands me. I understand her. We talk for hours. She accepts me for what I am."

He was so sure of himself that there didn't seem to be much more I could say at the time. I didn't want to undermine his new self-confidence. Yet I was aware of the frequent awkwardness in communication that would beset any long-term relationship between a deaf and a hearing person. The twins were determinedly independent, yet inevitably a hearing mate would have to be on call much of the time to interpret and explain. And while I liked to believe that love could bridge such a gap, I knew that marriage could be difficult enough without such an extra hurdle.

Finally, I knew the issue of marriage was linked to the general question of where Craig and Carson would, in the long run, feel most comfortable—in hearing or in deaf society. The choice of a mate would probably either determine, or be determined by, this larger choice, which neither Craig nor Carson had yet made. It was my own feeling that both of them would be happier married to an educated deaf girl, or perhaps to a hearing girl who was involved in the deaf world professionally; I had several times suggested this to the twins, but it was not something I could organize for them.

When Craig's girlfriend later visited our house, she and I sometimes talked privately, and we approached indirectly

131

the subject of Craig's deafness without ever spelling things out exactly. I knew it was an issue that concerned her.

In late winter the girl broke off her relationship with Craig. She told him it was partly because they came from different "backgrounds" and partly because he wanted to get serious too fast.

"I had the worst depression of my life then," Craig recalls. Although it was winter, he went camping alone in freezing weather, which seemed to match his emotional state. We were worried about him and went to Virginia later to see him. He would scarcely come out of his room.

Craig had always been something of a loner. Now he fell into that role again, still going to classes but casting hopeless glances at his former girlfriend when they met, and trying in solitude to understand what mistake he had made. He realized finally that he had in fact been too dependent on her, not so much as his interpreter but more as the sole focus of his social life.

He remembers, "I always wanted to be just with her, didn't want to be with other people. 'We don't need other people,' I thought. 'Let's just do something by ourselves.'" This impulse was certainly understandable, given the difficulty Craig had in following a conversation among a group of people.

But then, gradually, he realized that he had to be more open, even if sometimes this meant he would be lost: "I saw now that friends were very important. So I made myself go out and meet a lot of classmates." He was well-known at school and had been on the varsity soccer team, so contacts were available. "I did some dating but kept myself under control and didn't get too serious. And the end of that year was one of the best of my life up to that time."

All the rest of us in the family could sense in Craig a new self-assurance, which seemed to have a broader base than the high wave of young love he had been riding earlier in the year. After feeling as though he were in Carson's shadow for so long, Craig was now definitely standing on his own, within a large circle of friends.

Carson too had many friends, but the year as a whole left him with a new, perplexed awareness of the barriers between the deaf and hearing worlds. In two particular episodes the deaf world, which he had largely ignored, sought him out and forced him to confront his own deafness in a new way. He was sitting in class one day when a secretary interrupted and called him to the office.

"Someone just called from the county jail," he was told. "They have a deaf man there who speaks only sign language. They want you to come and interpret. Someone at Madison College gave them your name."

Carson drove to the jail. The jailer explained that they were holding the deaf man for drunken driving. He had been weaving his car over both lanes of a road the night before. "We want to tell him that if he gives us forty dollars for bail he can go home now," the jailer said.

The man in the cell was about 50 years old and wore shabby clothes.

"I'm here to interpret for you. My name is Carson Glick," Carson began to say in his formal signed English, but before he could finish, the man's hands exploded in a volley of signs that were completely bewildering to Carson.

Carson stood in his characteristically erect posture and signed with restrained, punctual movements, a little bit as though he were typing. The other deaf man, however, seemed to throw his hands about theatrically. His whole body twisted and his face grimaced as he described his misery in the expressive terms of American Sign Language.

Some of the few words Carson picked out of this storm of signs were "mother" and "home." No matter what Carson said, the perturbed man kept repeating that he wanted to go home to his mother.

"If you have forty dollars for bail, they will let you go home," Carson signed. The man didn't understand.

"Money," Carson signed. "Do you have any money?" The man got out his wallet, and they all counted the money. He had only twelve dollars. Immediately he began a tirade in signs again. The police had stolen some of his money, he said. He knew he had more than this.

"If you can't pay," Carson signed in his correct English word order, "you will have to stay overnight."

"I don't want to stay. They took my money...."

Finally Carson simply signed goodbye and turned to leave. The man's movements became almost threatening, and his face contorted as he mouthed a few unintelligible words. The jailer and Carson left him gesturing behind the bars.

Several months later the office at EMHS got another call for Carson, this time from a magistrate at the county courthouse. In an office there Carson met a middle-aged, motherly deaf woman, who looked much more respectable than had the man in jail. Carson's initial session as interpreter here, however, was almost as bewildering as his previous experience. This woman knew more English (she had been communicating with the magistrate by means of rudimentary handwritten notes), but when she signed, she too used "ASL": "The house ... the car ... can't go home ... clothing ... children ... left ... job finished ... he angry...." Frustrated by her tedious exchange of notes with the magistrate, the woman now let loose a barrage of signs, trying to tell Carson everything at once.

Only after several sessions with her did Carson finally understand that her husband had thrown her out of their house and would not let her return to visit her children or even to get her clothes. He had turned the children against her. He had denied her the use of their car. She was now living with a friend in a mobile home, sleeping on the couch and wearing her friend's clothes. She had recently lost her job. Her health was poor. She was trying to get back her share of the family possessions and custody of the children.

"I had never met anyone with so many problems," Carson says, "and I wasn't really ready to deal with some of them. For example, she was accusing her husband of adultery. But soon I got very involved personally; I took her problems on myself, and I got very moody and depressed." He served principally as an interpreter between the woman and her lawyer but also volunteered to help communicate with doctors about her illnesses.

Even after Carson and the woman had conversed a number of times, the language difficulties between them persisted. He remembers, "Especially when she got riled up, I'd always get lost. I had to keep asking, 'How is this related to that? Which came first?' It was only when I left, months later, that I really understood the sequence of everything that had happened to her."

Communication in spoken English with court officials and lawyers was also difficult for Carson because he was not familiar with legal terms and processes. He was thus struggling to understand both parties for whom he was expected to interpret.

The lawyer postponed his appointment with the woman five times. Finally a date was set for a hearing, and Carson and the woman worked hard to get her witnesses lined up for what they understood would be an effort to get some of her possessions back again.

When the hearing began, however, they realized that something was out of joint. The lawyers were discussing the custody of the children. There was no mention of possessions. Apparently Carson had misunderstood the lawyer. He and the woman were completely unprepared for the issue of custody and had brought the wrong witnesses! The case was decided against the woman. Since she was living in a friend's trailer, she had no place to keep the children, the court said. The woman was distraught.

"Don't worry," Carson tried to console her. "You can appeal to a higher court." However, an appeal was never made. The husband kept the children, and for at least as long as Carson was in contact with the woman, she was unable to regain any of her possessions. Now he looks back on the whole experience with considerable regret: "I was violating my ethical code as an interpreter, telling her what she could and couldn't do, being her advisor. The lawyer never suggested she could appeal. I gave her false hopes. As an interpreter I should never have gotten so involved personally."

The experience showed Carson the baffling world in which many deaf people live. For better or worse, it left him with a sense of many insurmountable "walls" between the deaf and hearing worlds. "There was the wall between the woman and her husband, the wall between her and her children, between her and me, between us and the hearing world," Carson remembers.

At school Carson was still successful both academically and socially. In his junior year he had been named a member of the National Honor Society. In his senior year he was elected vice-president of the student council. But he was feeling less self-confident in the limelight. "I knew more and more I could not pick up what was being said, what was happening. It was too complex. I didn't really want to be vice-president, but people pushed me and I wanted to make a name for myself. So I took it anyway."

The only public appearance Carson had to make was to deliver a welcoming speech when the president was sick;

and he did a good job. But in the student council itself he couldn't follow the discussion. "I was getting bored and was tired of being bored. People around me were getting better educated, more intellectual, but I couldn't take part in discussions because I didn't know really what they were saying. If I knew what was going on, I'd throw something in but most of the time I didn't. I was afraid of being laughed at if my remarks weren't appropriate."

Carson was never a quitter, however, and when his frustration had built to a high level, he decided to try his utmost to resolve it. He waited for a time when a group of six or eight students were talking together in a dormitory lounge and then joined in. "This time I'm really going to do my share of the talking," he thought.

"So I followed everything very quickly," he recalls, "and then I spoke before they could change the subject. I had the feeling people were reacting strangely to me, but I tried not to pay attention to that—I was so busy focusing on what was happening. I asked questions and made remarks. And I did follow most of what was happening. But when I went back to my room, I was exhausted. And I was not sure, thinking more about it—did I say the right thing? Did I really know what they were talking about? I had been so busy concentrating on the conversation I could barely remember afterwards what it had been about! My head began to ache, and I thought, 'I can't do this all the time.' "

I was not fully aware of Carson's frustrations at EMHS; if I had been, I could possibly have helped him more. But by this time the boys knew, and we knew, that they were to a great extent standing on their own feet. Although they still had serious problems and the miracle of healing had still not fallen from heaven, underneath it all there was finally a foundation. We all knew that in many respects the boys had "made it." They were able to take care of themselves and

Carson's senior picture, Eastern Mennonite High School, 1976.

138

Craig's senior picture, Eastern Mennonite High School, 1976.

Craig and Tina at the twins' high school graduation.

Carson and Tina at the twins' high school graduation.

had the means to work through, or accept, most of their own problems.

The twins were not overcome by any great feeling of accomplishment at the end of their high-school years. Both were eager to move on to the next school of their choice, Hesston College in Kansas. I suppose graduation exercises are often more significant for parents than for the students themselves. At any rate, as the occasion approached, I could tell it would be an emotional one for me. Because now, after so many years of worry, of looking ahead to the next challenge, of wondering whether in spite of the boys' progress they might still be dependent on us for the rest of their lives—now I finally could stop and see what had been accomplished.

As we traveled the familiar route to Virginia for the graduation weekend, I could feel the emotion building inside me. The occasion was further heightened by the arrival of Paul and Eva Rudy. Paul had been the boys' first teacher, the person who had heard the first crude sounds of speech— if you could call them that—which the boys uttered in their early, frantic years. Paul and Eva had been with us in St. Louis (where the boys broke the Rudys' window). Eva had panicked with me in the department store when Carson was lost. The Rudys came from West Virginia, but in a deeper sense they came from our past, and they sat next to Vernon and me at the front of the balcony in the chapel on graduation day.

I tried my best to be composed. When the black-robed figures marched in, we smiled a little at the differences between the once identical-looking twins. Carson was neat and proper, with his mortarboard at just the correct angle. Craig had a fuzzy beard and his cap was a bit off-center.

I even made it through the formal ceremony in which the diplomas were presented with only a lump in my throat.

And probably I would have been all right, when the honors were announced later, if the principal, Sam Weaver, had not unexpectedly said, "And now there are two seniors whom I would like to give a special award, because they have given so much to their class and to their friends. These are two young men who probably don't realize that I am talking about them now—Craig and Carson Glick."

Vernon and I looked down at the two heads we could recognize so well even under the black caps, and saw students on each side of Craig and Carson nudge them and gesture toward the speaker. The twins, who had not understood the principal, would find out only later what this was all about, and they would be grateful but not overwhelmed.

The unexpectedness of it all, however, really undid me. When the ceremonies were over, I was still crying and I wasn't sure how I was going to stop. I looked at Vernon and could tell that he, too, was moved. We looked at each other for a while, and each of us tried to say something. And then we just gave up on words altogether.

Chapter 12

Carson and a friend walked into the student-center lounge at Gallaudet College in Washington, D.C., sat down, and began talking and signing to each other at the same time, their signs keeping pace with the sentences they spoke in English. After several weeks of summer sign-language classes at the college, Carson's gestures now flowed more easily with his conversation.

He looked around the large room, where some 30 other deaf students were talking in small groups on the scattered sofas and chairs. Signs flew everywhere, charging the air with visual energy. Although Carson was used to a quiet world, this room was even quieter than usual. Few of the other people around him spoke aloud. Some mouthed words as they signed; others signed for a long time without pronouncing any words at all. From where Carson sat he could see many varieties of signed language, from finger-spelling to the most colloquial ASL.

Sign language comes in many forms, as Carson now knew. At one extreme end of the spectrum is finger spelling, which is not really a separate language at all but simply a (laborious) visual form of English. At the other end of the spectrum is American Sign Language (ASL), which is a dramatic language unrelated to English or any other spoken language. Between these two extremes are various forms of signed language which more or less follow the patterns of English. Most deaf people use all of these forms of gesture at times appropriate for each, and sometimes they will shift gears from one form to another in the same conversation.

At Gallaudet, the only liberal-arts college in the United States founded primarily for deaf students, Carson's teachers spoke and signed simultaneously. But he had found that in private conversations many students used some form of ASL and comparatively little speech.

The group on a sofa next to Carson burst into loud laughter—the less-restrained laughter of people who could barely hear the sounds they made. Startled by the sudden noise that jarred his hearing aid, Carson watched as the other students pushed each other and joked in a quick, colloquial ASL that seemed almost to mock the gestures of his slower, linear English sentences. Carson looked back at his friend with an expression that betrayed his disdain for the boisterous activity of the other group. He considered this kind of behavior to be one of the "deafisms" which he associated with less-educated deaf people. Carson wanted to avoid such stigmas at all costs. He was tempted to make some comment about the other group to his friend but thought better of it—you can't have a truly private conversation in signs because someone else, even on the other side of the room, can *see* what you say; and in a group of deaf people you can't tell who might after all be hearing, or might be especially adept at reading lips. So Carson fell back into his more restrained style of signing, with a set expression on his face, which could have been interpreted as a mark of either self-consciousness or arrogance.

"I went through a kind of culture shock that summer," Carson says of his first summer after high-school graduation. "Before I went to Gallaudet, I tended to look down on many deaf students because my English and general level of education were better. But when I got there, I found many people who were quite intelligent and who had something I didn't have—an easy way of communication."

Carson took one class in interpreting and another on teaching ASL. Both, it turned out, assumed a previous knowledge of ASL, so didn't greatly improve his proficiency in the language itself. Most of the other students in his classes not only were hearing but knew ASL better than he, so Carson was in a position of double disadvantage.

"Socially I still acted superior to many other deaf people at the school," he says now. "I pretended to be cool. I disliked many 'deafisms' I saw. I felt conversation was limited. Often deaf society is one or two years behind the hearing world, and at that time, when the drug scene was dying on most campuses, it was at its peak at Gallaudet.

"Still, at the same time, I wanted to be like them, or at least wanted to fit in and be more comfortable, wanted to be able to communicate better in ASL. I did pick up signs fairly quickly and saw how they were used. I didn't just see signs as symbols of something else anymore. I began to follow whole conversations for the first time—something I had never been able to do when people used only speech. When I'm with hearing people, I can never quite be comfortable because there is always the possibility that I'm not understanding. But at Gallaudet I could meet people, and we could talk about anything."

I had a good look at Carson's new proficiency in sign language later that summer when he was a co-teacher and I was a student at a sign language week at Laurelville, in western

Pennsylvania, where our church has a retreat center. Eli Savanick, a hearing friend of ours whose parents are deaf, was the instructor.

There was an air of adventure in the room when we 15 hearing members of the seminar met for the first time. Some were entering new territory and expected no doubt to acquire an almost secret, mysterious form of communication. I was a bit more apprehensive. I had taken an evening sign-language class before and had found my fingers to be just as awkward as had been the boys' first efforts to learn verbal speech. I had always encouraged them not to feel embarrassed by the mistakes they might make in speaking, but I must admit I suffered from a stage fright that stiffened my hands when I had to form a sign.

"Take these ear plugs," said Carson, "and keep them in your ears for the rest of the day." He signed as he spoke. "Rule number two," he continued. "After this introduction is over, you may not speak until we all get together again

Craig (left) and Carson at a family gathering.

this afternoon." There were gasps of dismay and Carson couldn't help smiling. Then he shook a finger at us. "Anyone caught talking will have to pay five cents a word."

We went outside. The earplugs made me feel as though I were underwater. I watched some children in the swimming pool across the lawn but couldn't hear their splashing. I stood in the driveway and laboriously finger-spelled my name to someone. I was watching my clumsy hands, and looked up suddenly and saw a car behind us. I hadn't heard the motor. I knew this experience wasn't really the equivalent of being deaf, but I was beginning to get the idea.

In the dining hall at noon Carson pointed to each kind of food on his plate and gave the corresponding sign. We all put down our forks and tried to imitate him. Our hands were so busy we seemed to have no time to eat.

By the end of our second day, in the discussion period, when we were allowed to talk, we all laughed and chatted away compulsively to release our frustration. I was certainly not the most adept learner, although perhaps neither was I the worst. One man broke down, yelled and banged his fist on the table because the coordination between his head and his hands seemed so awkward. Eli and Carson were both sympathetic teachers—but never hesitated to collect the fine for speech.

The scene I remember best from the week was a tennis game I played with Carson one hot afternoon. I could never remember how to sign the score. In my efforts to sign before each serve, I kept dropping the balls. Carson was patient. He would call me up to the net and repeat the signs, but by the end of the next volley I had forgotten again. In the midst of the fiasco, as perspiration collected on my forehead, I suddenly realized that this was just a hint of the way he had felt for years when he was learning to speak English.

I was happy to see Carson become proficient in sign language. My own contacts with deaf people and educators had by this time convinced me that sign would benefit any deaf person.

But Craig did not share Carson's interest in sign language. I let him know about my positive reaction to what I had learned about sign, but tried not to push him in this direction too obviously; I knew he would have to decide what his options would be concerning deaf society. Craig was eager to go to Hesston College in Kansas the next year and had made his decision about school independently of Carson, who also decided to attend Hesston. Craig had a summer job lined up in Kansas and planned to start soccer practice early.

Craig rode his motorcycle to Ohio, where we picked him up in our station wagon and took him out to Kansas. On the way, we talked more openly with him than we had before about the rivalry with Carson. He was quite articulate on the subject, partly because he had learned some things in a psychology course the year before, and we were pleased with his apparent independence from Carson at last. Unfortunately, perhaps, we assumed Carson was still as self-confident as ever, and were not quite aware of some of the disappointments he had suffered that year, or of the support he needed. The Jacob and Esau story had still not played itself out.

Soon after moving to Hesston College, Craig broke his ankle in a soccer game and had to come home for the summer. Disappointed, but convinced of the powers of positive thinking, he was determined not to be depressed. He thought that if he had the right attitude, his ankle would heal more rapidly, and—for whatever reason—the bones did knit back together in good time.

Both Craig and Carson went to Hesston in the fall. The

college put a strong emphasis on social life. Groups of students lived in small dormitory "mods" in close contact with each other. Every student belonged to a "D" (discussion) group that met twice a week for an hour or so. The emphasis, apt enough for Craig and Carson, was on communication. The problem as usual, however, was that communication in a large group was especially difficult for them. Topics discussed included "How to Be a Better Conversationalist" and "Body Language." Frustrated by his inability to follow what was said in group meetings, Craig developed his own "body language" vocabulary in which he could assert himself.

"In discussions, I couldn't follow what was going on, so I would often be mischievious and create disturbances," he recalls. "I might pick on another student, make gestures or faces until he would respond, and finally things would get out of control. I was self-conscious about what I was doing, but I did it anyhow."

Both Craig and Carson were persistent in their contacts with individual students and made friends quickly. Craig, however, had some problems in the first two mods where he lived, problems that were at least accentuated by his deafness. Where he first lived, four of the twelve members in the mod were black, and Craig had trouble reading both their speech and their culture. One evening two of the blacks were arguing vehemently about something a professor had said. Craig was perturbed by the fact that their violent disagreement was based only on hearsay. Finally, when he could stand the tension no longer, he got up and stood between them.

"Look," he said. "Stop arguing." His own face showed great perplexity. "If you really want to know what the professor said, go to him and *ask him*." The room quieted down immediately, and everyone shifted awkwardly. Craig went back to his room. His roommate soon followed.

"They argue like that all the time," the roommate said. "They weren't really angry at each other. They like to argue and exaggerate. It was mostly a joke."

In retrospect Craig now sees that he overreacted: "Because I couldn't hear, I wasn't able to pick up the cultural clues that would have told me they were just pretending to be angry."

The second mod Craig lived in had an even more colorful, if crude, variety of culture. It soon became apparent to Craig that he had been grouped with the "rowdies," whose sense of humor was about as subtle as a TV cartoon. One night someone picked the lock on Craig's door and threw a firecracker into the room. Craig didn't need his hearing aid to appreciate the prank. In an ensuing scuffle he threw the perpetrator against the wall and thereby earned a measure of respect from the group as a whole. This episode was only pe-

Craig at Hesston College, 1978.

ripherally related to Craig's deafness. Another incident was more pointed.

One night Craig came back to the dormitory and found that the rest of the mod was gathered in a meeting that he had forgotten was to take place. He joined the group. The matter to be decided was what nickname each mod member would bear on his T-shirt, scarcely an issue of international importance but in a small community significant enough.

"What do you want? Hurry!" everyone said. Craig couldn't think of anything. Embarrassed, he fumbled for words that could give him more time.

"How about 'Duh'?" said someone, glazing his eyes and pronouncing the word in classic "dumb" fashion. Everyone in the room hooted in amusement. Craig didn't know what had been said, but he knew he was the target and grew more embarrassed.

"How about 'Jock'?" someone else said. This was a reference to Craig's soccer and jogging. They all agreed immediately to this name, got up, and left without another word to Craig. A friend told him later what had been said in the meeting. He wore a "Jock" T-shirt that summer when he worked on a construction crew.

I mention this incident only because it was one of the few times when either Craig or Carson was subjected to the kind of ridicule that many deaf young people must endure. I do not wish to give a bad impression of Hesston College. In general, both Craig and Carson found the faculty and students there to be very responsive. In the other mods where Craig lived he made good friends, as did Carson. Both twins grew intellectually at the college. But the most notable increase in their perception seemed to come from their courses and independent reading in psychology.

When he read about how people react to loss, Craig finally seemed to understand the process he had gone through after his breakup with his first girlfriend: "I realized that everybody goes through steps of depression—shock, denial, depression, acceptance—and I had finally reached a point where I could accept life again." Interestingly enough, Craig did not apply his new tools of psychological analysis to his larger "loss" of hearing. To some extent it must have been because deafness had always been so much a part of him, was so close to him, that he couldn't distance himself from the issue and see it clearly. Or perhaps to face and fully accept his hearing loss would still have been too painful.

When the plane came down into the lights of Los Angeles at night, Carson felt exhilarated by what seemed to be the endless possibilities below him. Craig, on the seat beside him, was less excited. He would have preferred to come down over a forest instead.

Both twins characteristically had become somewhat restless at Hesston College and were now thinking of moving on to a different school, California State University at Northridge, where there is a special program for the deaf. At the airport they were met by four deaf students from the university, headed by a friend from Kansas, Lori Helferich.

Lori and her California friends greeted the twins animatedly, talking and signing at the same time. Carson was glad to see that they used mostly signed English instead of the ASL that was more common at Gallaudet. He began chatting fluently in signs himself. Craig, feeling more ill at ease, signed very little when he spoke.

They loaded a car with all the luggage Carson had brought in case he decided to stay for the next semester of school, and went up the freeways toward Northridge, 45 minutes away. As they traveled, Lori often turned on the light inside the car so that they could all read each other's speech and signs.

"Is this still L.A.?" Carson asked in amazement every ten minutes. He would continue to ask the same question for the next few days, as they traveled still further on the freeways, and he would always get the same answer, "Yes, of course." He realized he would not reach the boundaries of L.A. as soon as he had reached those of the other communities where he had lived. "I was almost hyper with excitement," he recalls.

The university itself offered plenty of room for him to exercise his energies. Physically the campus was expansive, and he was soon running a two-and-a-half mile course around part of its perimeter. Large blocks of lawn were laid out here around modern buildings. The library, a futuristic structure with huge carved columns, had been filmed in a TV series about adventures on another planet. The walkways were almost as wide as landing strips, and you could look down one to where it connected with a wide boulevard, which in turn went on for miles into the haze of L.A. in the distance.

The classes Carson visited at CSUN also offered new vistas. He was impressed by the high educational level of the deaf students he met, and found them to be quite independent. Each student had to find his own apartment and arrange for the necessities of life himself. Deaf students took regular courses with hearing students and were aided, on request, by both signing interpreters and notetakers. Course listings were voluminous. And for the first time, by watching the interpreters, Carson could follow almost everything that was said in class.

Vernon and I flew out to the school and were impressed. When Carson decided to stay, we concurred. Craig, who was less interested in sign language, elected to return to Hesston.

That spring was difficult for Carson. He had to find a roommate and get settled in a new apartment. He didn't have a car and without a car one is almost a nonperson in L.A. Finally, it happened to be one of the rainiest seasons in recent L.A. history. But if Carson felt a little lost in the expanses of California, he did enjoy its variety. In classes he was amazed at the torrent of opinions that flowed through the hands of the signing interpreters during open discussions. Seldom had he been in such active classes. In one American Government class of 60, there were students who were variously deaf, Jewish, foreign, and gay; some were intellectually well-developed, and others were from poor educational backgrounds. The teacher was a politically outspoken ex-priest, who had been an ambassador to Central America. Each cultural group in the class expressed itself forcefully. Carson absorbed and evaluated all these opinions. "I didn't argue, but I did ask questions—'What do you mean by that?' "

At the university Carson found a social group of deaf people with whom he felt comfortable. He was becoming more fluent in sign, he remembers: "It took me a while to adjust to signing as an only means of communication. At first I would get worn out easily. But after having a deaf roommate, I felt much more comfortable. Signs began to come out without my having to think what they were supposed to be."

Carson also began to understand better the workings of the "deaf community" and tried to adjust himself to its patterns. One thing he learned was how quickly the grapevine can transmit information there. "If a deaf student breaks a window out here one night," a friend of Carson's said, "by the next evening his parents in New York know all about it."

"Deaf people often seem more sensitive about what is said about them," Carson notes. "I was not considerate enough at first in talking about other deaf people." Once, for example, after Carson had an argument with his roommate, Ken, he told someone else about it, and by evening the story had circulated to Ken himself, who then follwed the trail back to Carson. "Ken was a big help in teaching me things about the deaf community," Carson says, and adds ruefully, "although I didn't always appreciate it."

Carson also made friends among hearing people in California. By this time his speech was good enough so that his pronunication could often be mistaken for some foreign accent. Usually when people found out he was deaf, they expressed admiration for his achievement. There was one notable exception. At a party with hearing people, Carson once met a man who was quite easy to understand, and after conversing a while Carson mentioned that he was deaf.

"The guy stopped, froze, started to say 'uh,uh,' with saucer eyes, and then he walked backwards away from me," Carson recalls. For a long time this episode disturbed Carson, until finally he discussed it with a friend, who said, "But what happened was *his* problem, not yours!" This remark settled the doubts in Carson's mind, and he continued to gain new confidence in himself. One day, in fact, he made his own direct reply to some of the prejudice he had encountered. He was standing in the midst of a group of students outside the university library.

"Look at those deaf people," someone near Carson remarked to a friend. "Don't they act strange?" The deaf people referred to were nearby, but the hearing students felt safe in talking about them loudly.

"They make strange noises."

"They always depend on other people."

Carson read these remarks on the lips of the speakers. Finally he walked over and confronted them.

"I know what you said," he announced. "I'm deaf, but I know what you said. It's not true. You don't know what it's like to be deaf. Don't judge other people." Embarrassed, the gossipers turned and stumbled away.

Since Carson was proficient in both speech and sign, Vernon and I had been encouraging him to go into an occupation in which he could serve as an intermediary between the deaf and hearing worlds. After he had served as interpreter for the deaf woman in Virginia, Carson himself had talked of becoming a lawyer for deaf people or of going into some kind of social work.

"I guess I felt I should do that, out of a Christian impulse, or whatever," Carson says now. "But it wasn't really what I wanted to do. I don't feel I need to rescue deaf people from the world. A lot of people who help deaf people have that attitude. I do want to become fluent enough in ASL so I can interpret for the deaf people around me, but I don't want to make a career of it."

He went through various plans for occupations, from social work to psychology to media communications to business and then, finally, to interior design. In the spring of 1979 he left school and, after some months of searching, found a job at Neiman Marcus, a large, exclusive department store. He enrolled that fall in courses in interior design at UCLA.

Craig enjoyed his last year at Hesston (a two-year junior college), living with more compatible roommates and continuing an active social life. When we visited once, it seemed he was constantly introducing us to friends. Craig, too, was vacillating in his choice of career. He became interested in a course in respiratory therapy and decided to try for a job in that field. There were no deaf respiratory therapists at St. Joseph's Hospital in Wichita, Kansas, where he finally applied for a position; in fact, there were possibly no deaf respiratory therapists anywhere in the United States, but the hospital agreed to try him.

By sight and touch Craig learned to distinguish the various kinds and degrees of "gurgling and wheezing and

157

rasping" that emerged from the patients' lungs. He circulated among patients who were recovering from pneumonia, emphysema, and bronchitis, and helped them with their breathing exercises.

"What nationality are you?" people often asked him.

"I'm from Pennsylvania," he would reply.

"Oh, so you're speaking Pennsylvania Dutch."

"No, I'm deaf, so I can't hear my accent."

"My biggest fear," Craig recalls, "was how patients would react when they learned I was deaf. I was afraid they might say, 'No, I don't want you to work on me.' But that was unjustified. They were all very understanding." Even one old lady who was at first uncooperative proved to be sympathetic in the end. She mumbled something.

"Pardon me, what did you say?" Craig asked.

"You talk funny!" she said accusingly.

"No, it is not that. It's just that I'm deaf," he explained.

"Her reaction was so sudden," Craig remembers. "She began to apologize profusely. I was holding a piece of equipment, and she kept grabbing me, trying to explain. I just kept saying, 'That's all right,' and could hardly get away."

Other staff members were all helpful. They made a special effort to alert Craig to anything important that came over the public address system. His hearing was so scant that he had some difficulty distinguishing the Code Blue call that signaled an emergency.

While he worked at the hospital part-time, Craig also worked 20 to 30 hours a week for a cement contractor. This was less interesting work, and Craig found it more difficult to talk to people on this job, he remembers: "I had to watch what I was working on all the time and couldn't look at the other workmen to see what they were saying. I missed most of their conversation. At the hospital I could look at people directly and talk to them."

158

After nine months at the hospital Craig decided that the routine of this job would become tiresome eventually. Like Carson, he took some time off and tried to get his occupational bearings. Finally he decided to go to Goshen College (affiliated with the Mennonite Church) in Goshen, Indiana, to study business. He moved there in the summer of 1979 to look for work, and got a job in a tool and die plant—driving a forklift—to earn his tuition for the next year.

So the twins' twenty-first birthday had come and passed; and gradually, without any official notice, our dreams had been realized. Craig and Carson were now to a great extent independent and could choose with great freedom what to do with their lives. Vernon and I had begun to develop our personal interests and felt the children could navigate their own courses. But we had forgotten something.

Chapter 13

Kristine Joy; Tina. She was an unusually happy baby, who, in contrast to her intense brothers, liked to cuddle in our arms. When she grew older, she added light and warmth to the family, as she darted from room to room in our big farmhouse or settled down in an armchair to play mother to Pepper's puppies. When the boys were at their most difficult age, Tina was a delight.

Why, then, when she was much older and the twins were finally on their own, did we get those phone calls late at night from Tina, unhappy calls for help interspersed with black silences, demanding that we turn back and reenact our family tensions all over again to allow a different role for her?

Tina was a junior at EMHS when Craig and Carson graduated, and on the whole she seemed to have a reasonably good year. When her brothers left for college in Kansas, however, and Tina was the only Glick at EMHS in her senior year, she fell rather quickly into a deep depression. The causes were many, and the phone calls we got from her at this time were not always coherent, but the central message came all too clearly over the night wires, "Nobody cares about me!"

"Of course we do!" we protested at first with some indignation, but this verbal reassurance didn't seem to have much immediate effect. Eventually we did demonstrate to Tina's satisfaction that we loved her, but it took a year or more, and it involved many discussions about certain family problems we had hoped were behind us.

Some of the things that troubled Tina were personal in nature, and some were related to aspects of our family life which I will not discuss here because they are not relevant to the topic of deafness. However, it is clear that some of Tina's problems were connected to her brothers' deafness. And I think many families with both handicapped and "normal" children are plagued with similar difficulties. On the simplest level, what happened in our family was that Tina, because she was "normal," sometimes received less attention from Vernon and me, and from other people, than did her handicapped brothers.

I can make the point best by describing a typical episode in the younger years of our family: We are on our way to visit the children's grandparents in central Pennsylvania. Tina is between Vernon and me in the front seat of the car, and the boys are in the back. Tina chatters on about what she wants to do on the farm: "Mom, can we go for a walk? Remember how we picked blackberries one time? Can we do that now? How will we know if there are any snakes? Remember the time...."

"How fah?" says Craig suddenly, loudly, in my ear, pushing against the seat impatiently. He can see that Tina is talking, cannot understand her words, and is now interrupting with at least some motivation of rivalry. I am dimly aware that his interruption is intentional, but I am so concerned about his learning to speak that I automatically turn so he can see my lips. "How far," I say, emphasizing the "r." "You want to know how far it is?"

"Yes."

"*Mama*," Tina shrills, "can we pick blackberries at Grandpa's? Will you go for a walk with me?"

"Just a minute," I say, then turn back to Craig. "Can you say, 'How *far?*' "

"How fah-r."

"Look!" Carson yells, wanting his share of attention. "Truck!" He balls up his fist in imitation of a truck that has passed us, pretends to drive it over the seat, and just nudges the back of Tina's head.

"Make him stop that, *Mama!*" Tina shrieks. "It's not *fair!*"

What ensues would no doubt be familiar to many families with three children competing for attention on a long trip. Indeed, the whole scene may not seem to have anything in particular to do with deafness. However, as over the years Tina was interrupted time and again by her brothers, and we often turned our attention to them, eager to encourage their speech, Tina felt she was being ignored and the boys were favored.

It's not that we obviously neglected Tina. She was the center of attention at home when the boys were at Pathway. When she was five years old, I took a trip to Florida with her alone so that we could be free of the tensions of the larger family. When the boys were home, however, we may have cheated her. We gave so much time to seeing that the boys understood, that they did their homework, that they didn't get killed outside. And Tina was always there, a little shadow sometimes, who didn't get the separate attention she needed.

The problem was not limited to our household. Other

162

people overextended themselves often in sympathy for the boys, and then if Tina showed any normal signs of competition, she was reprimanded. One elementary-school teacher described her in a report as a rather spiteful little creature, not at all like her diligent and obedient brothers. I'm sure that Tina's rebelliousness at school, in whatever ways it might have been expressed, was largely a reaction to the extra attention given to Craig and Carson, but no one thought of that.

As Tina grew older, she grew especially to hate the typical glowing conversations about her brothers that were imposed on her by friends of the family. Most of all, she says, "I had a hard time at family reunions. Everyone would say, 'Oh, hi, Tina, how are Craig and Carson? Where are they now? We're so proud of what they've done! Isn't it something!' Often people wouldn't even think to ask me about myself."

Craig and Carson themselves had a sense of self-importance, which was to some extent merely a symptom of

Tina as a child playing in the sandbox.

adolescence. They did have an additional element of self-righteousness, which was at least obliquely related to their deafness. Having worked so hard to achieve status in the hearing world, they could be intolerant of anyone who lacked discipline or violated their somewhat simplistic and rigid code of behavior. Tina almost deliberately became more lax in her habits just to demonstrate her independence.

To show a typical conflict situation between her and the twins, I have drawn a scene from their early high-school years: Craig and Carson are studying in their basement room, completely absorbed in their books, which lie in circles of illumination cast by their high-intesity desk lamps. They are mumbling faintly as is their custom when alone. Then Craig begins to whistle the loud tuneless notes that so often accompany the boys' studying. They always whistle the same notes, over and over, notes whose frequencies reverberate somewhere within the range of sounds they can hear. To the twins it is a soothing sound they like to repeat for hours at a time. The effect on Tina is much like the feeling a cat apparently gets when its fur is rubbed systematically the wrong way. Tina usually endures the whistling as long as she can and then asks them to please stop. They generally shrug, stop, and then later, never really aware of how far the sound carries, start up the same monotonous, mournful notes again.

On this night Vernon and I are at the store. Tina is upstairs looking at her own homework. She soon comes down to her brothers' open door and looks in at the bent heads, straight backs, and nervously vibrating legs that mark their typical posture for study. Knowing it is no use to knock or call their names, she goes in and touches Craig on the shoulder. He looks up, indignantly.

"I can't study while you whistle," Tina says. Craig doesn't, or pretends not to, understand. Tina knows his hear-

164

ing aid is turned off. He doesn't turn it on.

"Stop whistling, *please*," she points to her mouth. Craig looks back at his book. Exasperated, Tina goes upstairs and sits down at her own books. The whistling begins again. She stalks into our bedroom, locks the door, and turns on the TV, the volume almost loud enough to drown out the whistling, but she is also glad for an excuse not to study. Her study habits and her life in general are not as disciplined as her brothers'. In fact, after hearing them praised so often for their academic accomplishments, she is determined not to compete with them for grades. She never reads books voluntarily. In so many ways she wants to be different from them, no matter what.

Half an hour later there is a loud knock on the bedroom door. She makes no answer.

"I know you're in there," Craig says. "You know you're not supposed to watch TV until you do your homework."

Carson and Craig with Tina.

165

Fifteen minutes later there is another knock. "You're not supposed to watch TV yet," Carson calls. "I'll tell Mom."

After the program is over, Tina opens the door and goes into the kitchen. Craig and Carson are drinking glasses of milk. Tina avoids their stares and pours some milk, gets down a can of cocoa mix and heaps chocolate into her glass.

"Chocolate isn't good for you," says Carson. "It gives you pimples."

"I don't have any."

"It makes you fat," says Craig.

"Fatso," says Carson.

"I'm going to call Mom; you're awful." Tina goes toward the phone. The boys catch her and push her away. They form a barrier around the phone.

"Don't try to tell me what I can and can't do," Tina yells. "You're always trying to boss me around. Why can't you let me?..."

In the middle of her tirade the boys both turn off their hearing aids and look away, while Tina bursts into tears. There is no way that her anger can penetrate the deliberate silence they have thrown up against her. This silence was the one unusual power that Craig and Carson could exercise. They could literally tune someone out when they wanted to.

Still, they depended on the rest of the family to help them understand the larger world. Since Tina was often with them, she was frequently called upon to serve as interpreter, to explain why everyone was laughing in a group at school, to ask girls for dates on the phone, to explain what was happening on TV. It was virtually impossible for Tina to get absorbed quietly in a TV show because her brothers, who could understand almost none of the dialogue, constantly interrupted her. The following scene is typical of what often took place in the TV room:

"What did he say?" asks one of the twins.

166

"He asked where the money was," Tina responds.

"What money?"

"The money the other guy stole."

"What other guy?"

"The one with the striped shirt."

"With what?"

"The *striped* shirt." Tina gestures to show stripes.

"Who is the woman?"

"She's.... Can't you wait a minute? I can't hear what they're saying," says Tina. The boys wait, but she is absorbed in the dialogue and doesn't volunteer any more information.

"What did he say now?"

"Just *wait* a minute, can't you!" she says in exasperation. While at first she had good intentions and didn't mind interpreting, now the story is moving too fast for her to interpret and follow the action simultaneously.

After a while one of the boys throws a pillow, which bounces off Tina's head. She flashes a look of anger at him and then slumps out of sight into her chair. The phone rings and she goes to answer. The boys try to read her lips and can't.

"Who was it?" they both ask when she comes back. She simply watches the TV in silence.

"Who was it? What did they want?"

"It wasn't for you."

"It's not fair. We can't hear it. You can."

"It wasn't for you; that's all you need to know." Thus, Tina could use the power of silence too.

We asked a lot of Tina at times, in that we expected her to subordinate herself to the twins' needs or understand *their* frustrations. Ironically, however, in other respects we didn't ask as much of Tina as we did of her brothers. After exhausting ourselves to make sure the boys did their homework and understood everything, we tended to let Tina slide by at school, and I didn't even ask her to help with housework as much as I would have if she had been the only child. It seemed easier to just do it quickly myself. In a way, of course, our asking less of Tina was also a form of neglect.

Most poignant of all, Tina picked up a comment she overheard, and misinterpreted it to reflect her own feelings of being unwanted. She tells me, "One of you said that if you had known the boys were deaf you wouldn't have had me. I took that to mean you didn't want me."

Like most young children, Tina was not able to clearly articulate her frustrations at an early age. She does remember that once when she was quite small, she yelled in anger at her brothers, "You're deaf!" The remark was overheard, and she was administered a swift spanking. Tina, even at that time, felt she deserved the punishment, but I wonder if there might have been a better way to deal with her anger. A friend of mine also has a deaf child and a hearing child, and the latter sometimes says of her deaf sister, "I hate her."

"I hate *it* too, sometimes," the mother responds, referring to the fact of deafness, thus making it possible for the child to transfer and share the anger.

Above all, I wish we had talked more with all our children about some of the things that troubled them. I often failed to do this, because I thought, perhaps correctly, that they wouldn't understand my words. I think now it is a mistake not to talk to someone because you assume he won't understand. This thought, after all our years of stretching the boys' vocabulary, brings me to a somewhat different view of talking itself: if you talk, the concern will show on your face, at least, and sometimes that is more important than the words you say.

One of Tina's earliest childhood memories is of trying to

168

call her brothers: "They were out in the barn playing, and you asked me to go out and get them. I went outside the door and yelled and yelled. I just couldn't understand why they wouldn't hear me. I thought, 'Maybe this time they will!' So I called again. Then finally I went out and got them."

As in this early scene Tina did, throughout her years with Craig and Carson, often "go out and get them." She did often serve as their translator. She was never really embarrassed by their being deaf.

"I knew I could count on Tina's help if I really needed it," Carson recalls. "It was a big help to me psychologically." He remembers one episode on the school bus, when Tina got involved in a loud argument with some other children, which he couldn't understand: "Tina was crying when we got off the bus, and she told Mom that the kids had made some remark that we were dumb! I asked Tina what was wrong and she told me. I was glad to know she stood up for us."

In high school also, Tina was always ready to defend her brothers when she sensed that anyone else was slighting them. She recalls that "Craig and Carson had friends—two sisters. The older one was dating someone with a leg brace. The mother didn't want marriage for fear her grandchildren would be handicapped. I asked the girl whether her mother would feel the same way about Craig and Carson. She said yes. I was so mad. I hardly knew what to say to tell her off properly. I thought she was so shortsighted."

As the children grew older, they shared several important religious experiences. One of these made Tina feel closer to Craig, even though he was unaware of her presence. "I heard these strange sounds downstairs," Tina remembers, "and I went down. They seemed to be coming from Craig's room. I went to his door slowly and saw him standing in the middle of the room praying, with his eyes shut." His intensity held her for a while; then she left quietly, with mixed feelings of having intruded and of having shared something private.

When Carson went to Virginia during his junior year and Craig and Tina were left together at home, they drew somewhat closer together. Tina tried to help Craig get out of his depression and become more active socially. She recalls a most important occasion for her: "When I was baptized into the church, we could pick anyone we wanted to assist, and since Craig and I had been home together and been close, I asked him to help baptize me." Craig poured the water into the hands of the pastor who performed the ceremony.

At EMHS when the boys were seniors and Tina was a junior, she remembers them as being warmer and more brotherly toward her: "Carson had been there first and had scouted the way. Now I could ask him for help more, and he made me feel at home down there. They both became more protective of me in a more understanding way and didn't

The twins and Tina at Harrisonburg, Virginia, in 1977.

pick on me all the time anymore. I was associated with them in the minds of other people, and I guess that was one time when it was okay. People would always say such nice things about them. After a while that got a little annoying again but not too bad. On the whole there was more affection between us."

All three were in one course together, a Christian Family class. One assignment was to ask their parents questions about family history: what their parents had been like as children, how they got together, and what their early married life was like. Our family met one afternoon, and Vernon and I answered the childrens' questions as best we could. It gave us all a sense of solidarity. The children were especially affected by Vernon's account of his own past. "I remember when Dad said, 'I was not a happy child,' and he said it so quietly," Craig recalls, "and I was surprised by that. I had never known. And he said he had always wanted to get more education but had not been able to. I felt sorry for him but also had a great admiration for him because he had been successful without much education. That's a feat! And I remember your saying you wished you had talked more about your past before getting married, so you would have a better idea about what it would be like."

Our family problems were far from solved at this time, but the fact that we could talk more openly was a positive note. And whatever rivalries were still brewing in the minds of all three siblings, whatever anger would still explode from Tina, especially in the next year, there was one sign of family strength that we all laughed about.

Each student in the Christian Family class had been asked to draw a diagram which would show his interpretation of the various relationships in his family. When Tina, Craig, and Carson held up their respective diagrams for the class to view, it was quickly apparent that each of them had placed

171

himself as the dominant figure in the middle of the page!

It was after her brothers left for Hesston, Kansas, when Tina was alone at EMHS in her senior year, that she began to feel a new and curious kind of depression taking hold of her. "I went to visit Craig and Carson at Hesston," she recalls, "and when I got back, I cried and cried, because I could see they were doing so well without me! They seemed happy and I wasn't happy. I think in some ways I felt motherly toward them, and I was hurt when they didn't need me anymore."

Tina's relationship with her brothers had always been ambivalent: she enjoyed the sense of importance she received as their sister, yet resented their frequent dominance; she liked to feel they depended on her help, yet she wanted more freedom to be herself. Now her reactions to their departure were mixed as well. On the one hand, she began to follow her own inclinations more rather than react to her

Carson and his mother, Ferne Pellman Glick, at Tina's graduation from Eastern Mennonite High School.

brothers' reputations; for example, after years of having scorned their studiousness, she now began to read more and discovered the pleasure of books on her own. On a deeper level, however, she felt lost, and her old feelings of having been ignored now surfaced with surprising explosiveness. She began to express her frustrations, and throughout the next two years we got the long-distance phone calls which I mentioned earlier.

We made frequent trips to Virginia to talk with Tina, and gradually her emotional state improved. She moved back with us while waiting for an assignment under the Voluntary Service program of our church. After her anger had burned off, after she was reassured of her place in the family and felt more independent, Tina did not really seek complete liberation from her past. Rather, she wanted to redefine some of her old roles. She wanted to work with handicapped people, especially retarded children!

The whole family (left to right): Carson, Ferne, Tina, Craig, and Vernon Glick.

"Certainly my experience with my brothers gave me an interest in helping handicapped children," she says. The twins also helped her make contact with other handicapped children. Tina remembers particularly the first time she met retarded children, at a camp where Carson was a lifeguard: "When I was scared of them, Carson would always try to make me feel comfortable. He helped me not to be afraid of them."

Tina spent a year at home during which she worked as a secretary, waiting for an assignment, which finally took her to Baltimore, where she worked with retarded adults. And, not surprisingly, I suppose, she eventually became most interested in those retarded persons who were also deaf.

Chapter 14

In August of 1980 our family took a trip together back to Alberta. We stayed for a while with Vernon's brother's family in Edmonton and then made a one-day trip to Calling Lake. Tina was 21, and we thought this was a fitting time to return to her birthplace.

The road from Athabasca to Calling Lake was still unpaved for part of the way, and we drove through rain showers and mud. The area seemed just as remote as it was in 1959 but somehow more drab, more monotonous, than we had remembered, with mile after mile of scrub trees and undergrowth. Our arrival in Calling Lake itself was scarcely momentous. We splashed through the streets—which were really just several loosely associated dirt roads in the brush—and stopped at the local general store for information. With some uncertainty we then located the vacant spot where our house had been; it had burned down long ago. And even the sawmill where Vernon had worked was gone. We were vaguely excited but couldn't seem to make a connection with anything recognizable from our past. And when we stopped in Athabasca to locate the records of Tina's birth, only to find they had been either destroyed or misplaced, our general feeling that this part of our lives was far behind us seemed to be confirmed.

I don't think any of us were particularly disturbed by this experience, however. We were all leading reasonably fulfilling lives in the present and were glad that those early troublesome years were gone. When we had bumped out of Calling Lake 20 years before, there had been many bitter silences in our family life. Now, while we scarcely claimed to be models of sweetness and consideration, at least we understood each other better.

One example of this improved communication stands out in my mind. During our trip we stopped to visit friends whom we hadn't seen for a long time, and when we left the home, the woman said with great feeling, "I'm so glad you stopped; I wanted so much to see the boys again." The remark was made to Vernon, Tina, and me. I saw a pained expression come over Tina's face. She turned on her heel and walked to the car. Here, on a trip in her honor to the place where she had been born, she was faced with what to her was the same old insult she had endured for so many years—praise for her brothers and seeming indifference to her. The situation was particularly ironic in that the remark was not made in the presence of the twins, who thus received no pleasure from the compliment. As usual, to the sensitivities of Tina it seemed almost as though the comment about her brothers was designed merely to make her feel bad.

Of course it wasn't. The friend was well-meaning and the remark, if unthinking, was innocuous; but Vernon and I both knew immediately how it would strike Tina, and we talked to her about it later. I don't remember exactly what we said, but the fact that we said anything in sympathy made a great difference to Tina. When she realized that we had sensed her reaction and had seen the look on her face, the sting of the occasion was largely removed for her.

In their relationships with each other by this time, Tina, Craig, and Carson were also more at ease. They respected each other more, because each had shown him or herself to be a strong and independent person. There were occasional eruptions of the old stubborn patterns of rivalry on the Alberta trip and again during our next visit together back home the following Christmas; but there was a difference now in that everyone was much more aware of the emotional forces that set these scenes in motion.

"Christmas vacation [1980] was good for us," says Tina. "At first the twins and I would fight sometimes like we used to, and then we realized how much we had always miscommunicated and had talked past each other." All of us by now were trying to step out of the old unconscious roles we had played before in the family.

The twins had been independent to a large degree for several years by this time. Tina, however, had more recently left the nest and the old neighborhood. She had chosen a turbulent place in which to test her wings, and proved to have more strength than she herself had suspected. In the summer of 1980 she worked as an aide in a home for 36 retarded adults in Baltimore. "I didn't learn a lot there in a textbook way," she says, "but I did learn a lot about how to communicate."

She took the retarded clients to the shore, supervised other recreation, and was in daily close contact with them. Suddenly, "I became a voice of authority," she says. "I was ripped around emotionally. They might be very affectionate one minute and then throw fists and say, 'I hate you,' the next. I was like a board they would slap things up against, so I had to be more steady. They had a simple innocence, and I don't mean that negatively. They wouldn't respond to the usual head games and would say exactly how they felt." At the same time, "Many of them were so good at manipulation, because that worked for them so well for so long. They kept me on my toes."

In the sometimes exaggerated emotional expressions of these retarded people, Tina began to perceive all too obvious parallels with certain patterns she remembered in herself and her brothers: "I see now that at home I often threw tantrums without knowing why, and I know the twins threw tantrums when they were trying to express something else."

The joke was thus really on us when we laughed and said that Tina's experiences at home had been ideal training for her career in helping the retarded. And when we laughed at some of the stories Tina brought back from Baltimore, it was in sympathy with the clients, not at their expense.

While it is certainly cruel to make fun of any handicapped persons, there is a kind of humor that gives handicapped persons relief from their condition. In fact, one of the benefits Tina felt she got from her contact with the clients in Baltimore was an improved sense of humor. They were often the first to laugh about the absurdities of their lives.

One client who had a particularly good sense of humor was Sammy (not his real name), who was deaf as well as retarded. He was affectionate, always trying to get people to laugh, and Tina developed a close relationship with him. They communicated to some extent with signs, but, as Tina says, "with mentally retarded people it's not so much what you say as how you say it. It was often my eyes that would communicate with Sammy when my signs were wrong."

Sammy seemed reasonably happy, and it was thus something of a shock to Tina and the rest of the staff and clients when one day Sammy tried to hang himself. Tina arrived at the scene immediately after the incident and was quite disturbed by it. Sammy survived but was taken away from the home and placed for a while in a locked hospital room. No one ever really understood why Sammy had committed this act of desperation. It seemed possible that in part he simply didn't understand the seriousness of what he had done. He was an avid watcher of children's cartoons on TV, and the staff speculated that perhaps Sammy thought he, like Roadrunner, would simply emerge unscathed in the next scene. Still, there was obviously a deeper motive in Sammy's mind, and Tina's contact with this near-tragedy left her with a new concern for people like Sammy. Her involvement with handicapped people was stronger but less compounded with pity after that summer. And the intensity of her experiences burned away also certain elements of self-pity and self-indulgence.

In the fall of 1980 she took a year-long job at a church-sponsored home for retarded adults in Washington, D.C., and lived in a house with other young people in a ghetto neighborhood. Here the tragicomic elements of life were even more intense; in a few short months Tina was attacked on the street for no apparent reason, a friend was raped, other incidents of violence occurred in the area where she lived, she put her foot through a window while rescuing a cat, and her car was impounded twice—all this in addition to the strains of work.

But as I listen to her voice on a tape cassette now (in the fall of 1981), I am struck by how strong and confident Tina sounds. She is planning to return home soon to continue college work in special education. "I'm more aware now, more opinionated in a good way," she says. "I used to think being opinionated was a bad thing because Craig and Carson were so strong-minded and stubborn, and I felt like hitting them, but now I see it more as a positive thing to have strong ideas—if you know what you're talking about ... I think things through more now; I feel good about myself."

So I have been forewarned! When Tina moves home again, I'm sure I will have a difference of opinion on how well-thought-out some of her ideas are. But I'm sure now there will be more genuine dialogue than there used to be in our family. Painful and dangerous as it may seem sometimes, I do want my children to have their own ideas. It's good I feel that way, I suppose, because all three have clearly gone their own individual ways.

Craig is still at college in Indiana, taking business courses and, perhaps a little incongruously, dreaming of a life that is more self-sufficient. He spends much of his spare time gardening and canning and freezing his produce. When we visit him, he shows us his jars of preserves on the shelf. He is conservative by nature, more interested in tradition perhaps than Carson but just as determined to push himself to his limits. His friends are largely in the hearing world, but Craig is beginning to use interpreters somewhat more as backup to ensure communication. And he gets through to people in his own way. I notice how often he gives the world a slow, warm smile.

Carson is a world away in Los Angeles, deftly threading his way at high speed over the freeways, working in an exclusive department store and studying to become an interior designer. When we visited him last, he was at work in the gift gallery of the store, among the expensive china, crystal, and linens. One crystal eagle cost $16,000.

"Do me a favor," I said. "Don't touch that." He laughed, "I move it all the time." And in fact he moved through this crystal worth thousands of dollars with total confidence.

People knew him, and someone told us how Carson had gotten the inventory straightened out; and when the girl in sports said, "Oh, we love Carson," he got red. Carson is vulnerable too despite his air of self-possession.

He was always very sensitive to the moods of things, and his interest in interior design makes sense. As I think about his childhood, I can see his awareness back then of interiors, of light and shadow. After all the rooms and corridors, the windows and doors, that sometimes opened and sometimes stayed closed in his remembered past, Carson wants now to create an order for himself. "I like light," he says.

At the close of this story I would like to address directly several issues which have been left hanging thus far. In particular there is one word which comes up frequently in talk about handicapped children and their education, a word I would rather avoid but somehow feel I must face. This is the word "success." Was an educational method "successful"? we want to know. Was such and such a handicapped person "successful" in adapting to society or in overcoming his limitations or in achieving a "normal" life? Thus even in my own mind, I suppose, there lurks the question of whether Craig and Carson could be described in terms of this kind of success.

It is certainly true that Craig and Carson have learned to speak and read speech with greater proficiency than most other profoundly deaf people. They can carry on conversations with hearing persons on any topic, especially if the other person takes some pains to enunciate clearly and doesn't mind repeating himself occasionally. Their speech is fairly easy to understand, and their "accent" is not readily identifiable, giving them a slight air of being foreigners who are nonetheless fully conversant in English. For this ability our family is certainly grateful, because, as one commentator says, "It is an unfortunate fact that most deaf persons have unintelligible speech." *

---

* Hans Furth, *Deafness and Learning: A Psycho-Social approach* (Belmont, Cal.: Wadsworth Publishing Co., 1973), p. 18.

Of course one wonders immediately why Craig and Carson have been so successful in learning speech. I must confess I don't know. I certainly give thanks to the good teachers the twins had. At the same time, I emphatically do not see the twins' speech as proof of the validity of any particular educational method. I saw enough other "aphasic" children who were subjected to the erstwhile McGinnis Method to know that it was no magic formula, and I have talked to enough deaf persons who received even better oral educations to know that oral schools do not often produce clear conversant speech in their profoundly deaf graduates. Craig and Carson are not evidence in favor of any oral method. Nor does intelligence explain their aptitude. I have met very intelligent, well-educated deaf people who received extensive therapy in speech and whose spoken language is nonetheless almost unusable.

It would seem likely that Craig's and Carson's success in speech is due partly to some innate talent which is separate from intelligence. A number of researchers have emphasized recently that the ability to speak and read speech among deaf people may be in part a hereditary trait, like an ability to draw or play music. Another possibility is that what little residual hearing Craig and Carson possess is somehow more usable to them. Loss of hearing is rarely just a simple reduction in volume. There are innumerable other variables involved, such as the frequencies that can be detected, and additional forms of distortion exist whose nature can only be guessed at by a hearing person.

We used to say to other people that what the boys heard was like a very distant radio station out of tune, that would emerge, fade, and crackle with static so that an increase in volume was useful only up to a certain point. This analogy may help to illustrate that the kinds of sound reception in deaf people can vary greatly. Thus it is possible that Craig

182

and Carson have a kind of hearing loss which is slightly less disadvantageous than some other kinds. All this is mere speculation, however, and not something that has been detected by any audiologist Craig and Carson have seen.

Rather than puzzle fruitlessly over the possible reasons for the twins' success in oral speech then, I would rather look more closely at the concept of success itself, as this word is used to describe the achievements of handicapped, particularly deaf, persons. Obviously oral speech alone is not a very reliable measure of success. If it were, all of us who have normal speech would be successful.

I think that when we desperately hopeful parents of deaf children dream of their future, we are almost as concerned about social adjustments as we are about speech. We want our children to interact confidently with their peers and to eventually find their places in the larger society. To return to my own family, I must say that here again we seem to be fortunate. Craig and Carson can live in and interact with hearing society to such a degree that they can reasonably consider a range of occupations from business to medicine to law to forestry.

However, in the midst of all the apparent achievement, I hope it will not be taken as ingratitude if I point out the limitations, because there were certainly parts of our story which could have been improved upon, and I feel a certain compulsion to face the rather discouraging question of what I would do differently if I had another deaf child in my arms.

At the risk of repeating myself I would emphasize again a point I have raised before: We had more silences in our family than those created by deafness, silences which were painful and often unnecessary. Vernon and I had to learn a language of emotion, to understand both ourselves and each family member more fully. Thus, even if the twins' command of language had been normal, we would have had problems with communication. If I were to live through the experience of raising a deaf child again, I would be more concerned to keep all forms of communication open. I would hope to have a more relaxed attitude, and am optimistic enough to think that this would help, not hinder, the acquisition of language generally.

Second, I must repeat my earlier observation that the use of sign language would have made things easier. I think of all the frustrations in the boys' younger years, when we couldn't even say, "We'll be gone for an hour; then we'll come back." All we could do was leave and listen to their bewildered crying. I think with dismay also of all the talk they missed on the playgrounds and in their classrooms through the years. And I think of the fact that they continue to understand very little of what is said when they are in groups of people. In a school (or home) where sign language was used by everyone, they would have been able to understand much more of the immediate language environment.

Many educators tell us that use of sign language in conjunction with speech has no bad effect on the learning of oral language. I am inclined to believe this but would like to pose a theoretical question. Suppose the ideal situation broke down, and the use of sign language did slow a deaf child's acquisition of speech to a moderate degree. Might it still be best to sacrifice a measure of oral ability in order to give the child a means of really full and easy communication? Would such a child, talking fluently among family and friends in sign, be less successful than one who learned oral language slightly better but struggled constantly to communicate and missed much of the conversation around him?

I would raise a similar question concerning social success. Would a young deaf person whose social life was almost exclusively within the bounds of the "deaf community," and who felt at ease among deaf friends with whom he could converse easily—would this "limited" deaf person be less successful than his oral counterpart who cultivated a few oral friends but was troubled by never quite feeling at home with them?

I don't pretend that the answers to these questions are easy. I do want to point out that it is ridiculous to define the success of a deaf person in terms of his oral ability and that oral ability often has little to do with happiness or well-being in general. I have met many deaf people in recent years who have little oral speech but enjoy full and expressive lives through sign and written language.

It would be presumptuous of me to attempt to evaluate whether or not Craig and Carson are happy in their present social situations and whether they would be happier elsewhere. From my point of view they are now somewhat marginal figures, located between deaf and hearing societies; they themselves might not agree with this view of their respective situations. Wherever they go, I hope at least that I will measure their success by their ability to communicate in the broadest sense.

As I make these pronouncements, however, I feel a bit uneasy—and probably I should. When I was talking in a similar vein to a hard-of-hearing friend of ours once, he bristled and cut me short: "It's easy for you to say that parents should use sign and accept their deaf kids for what they are. Your kids 'made it' in the traditional sense. You never had to face what some parents do."

But there is an even better reason why I should hesitate to pontificate about deafness and the deaf community. I do not know what it is like to be deaf. I can never understand even what Craig and Carson live with. Thus, while I might occasionally speak of accepting deafness, I must realize that these easy words gloss over a complex of emotions and hard situations which Craig and Carson cannot dismiss so easily. For example, it surprised me recently to discover that both twins still hope someday to be "healed."

As Craig and Carson described their feelings about this more fully, in separate conversations, I was reminded again that there is no end to the process by which a deaf person adjusts to his deafness. The feeling of loss is always there—somewhere—for Craig and Carson. Yet deafness is such a part of them that in a curious sense its removal would be a denial of themselves.

Carson repeats a story he has heard from his deaf friends. When deaf people suddenly have their hearing restored by surgery, he claims, they sometimes suddenly "go crazy" under the new barrage of stimuli and beg their doctors to reduce their hearing again. Thus, Carson thinks, maybe he shouldn't look forward to complete hearing after all.

Craig, too, has a vague fear that having his hearing suddenly made whole would be threatening, that he might lose control, "do anything," "conform to everybody else." His deafness, it seems, is a part of his personality which makes him feel independent and gives him objective distance from the world.

So, Craig says, he returns to the assurance that God knows best and to his habitual method of dealing with frustrations: "When I get frustrated again and again, often it comes back to me, 'I'm deaf,' and I think, 'I want to be healed! I want to hear! I want to hear now!' So I do something to try to forget this. I talk to someone, pray, give it up to God, or try to succeed at something I never did before. I might get a new job or try to make new friends. Or sometimes I just go to new places alone, try to understand perfect strangers, ask people, 'How do I get there?' or 'What time is it?'

"I guess," he pauses, "I guess I just need something to overcome."

When I hear Craig say this, I realize I don't actually

understand what deafness is and how it feels to him. And I find it harder to use the cliché of accepting deafness."

Thus, while I hope through this book to be of some help to parents of deaf children, anything I say can only be a starting place. I certainly advise families with deaf children who are bewildered by their situation, to go and talk with those who really know what it is like to be a deaf child. Go and "talk"—in speech, writing, or whatever method can be used—with deaf adults. If there is initial difficulty in communicating with these people, you might as well get used to it. You will be communicating with deaf people the rest of your lives.

Those of us who are hearing need to make the first move to penetrate the silence of the deaf world, especially those of us who have deaf children. For me, one of the strongest images of this necessary step is Tina's early memory of trying to call her brothers home from play, and finally having to go to where they were and literally reach out with a touch or gesture they could understand.

"I went outside the door and yelled and yelled. I just couldn't understand why they wouldn't hear me. I thought, 'Maybe this time they will!' So I called again. Then finally I went out and got them."

Ferne Pellman Glick was born in Richfield, Pennsylvania, and grew up there in a large farm family of eight. She and her husband Vernon now live in Lancaster, Pennsylvania, where they settled with their three children (Craig, Carson, and Tina) following several years in Newfoundland and Alberta, Canada.

Ferne has long been associated with her husband in Glick Audio, Inc., an audio sales business. In 1978 she and a partner started two clothing stores, one of which (Next to New) still occupies much of her time.

She has been active in organizations within the Mennonite Church and her community, especially several that provide services for the deaf. She is a member of the advisory committee for deaf ministries of Mennonite Board of Missions, Elkhart, Indiana, and is vice president of the board for the Hearing Conservation-Deaf Services Center in Lancaster.

Mrs. Glick is a graduate of Eastern Mennonite High School, Harrisonburg, Virginia. She and her husband are members of Akron Mennonite Church, Akron, Pennsylvania.

Donald R. Pellman, a cousin of Ferne Pellman Glick, the coauthor of this book, was born in Harrisonburg, Virginia. He and his wife, Manon Larin Pellman, live at Franklin, Vermont, with their son, Nathaniel.

Pellman is employed as a law clerk by Peter J. R. Martin, Esq., St. Albans, Vermont, involved in legal research, writing of briefs, case investigation, and drawing up pleadings.

He is a graduate of Eastern Mennonite College, Harrisonburg, Virginia, and holds an MA degree from Columbia University, 1967. He taught high school and college English literature for six years before beginning his legal profession.

His articles on rural life have appeared in *Country Journal*, *Yankee Magazine*, and *New York Times Magazine*.